EXODUS

THE GREAT DELIVERANCE

E. G. WHITE

 **Remnant**
Publications

EXODUS
THE GREAT DELIVERANCE

Remnant Publications, Inc., Coldwater, Michigan
© 2014 by Remnant Publications, Inc.
All rights reserved. Published 2014

Printed in the United States of America

ISBN: 978-1-629130-56-9

Cover and interior design by Remnant Publications, Inc.,
Coldwater, Michigan

Compiled from the original works of E. G. White:
Patriarchs and Prophets and *The Great Controversy*.

God Hears the Cries of His People

And the Lord said: "I have surely seen the oppression of My people who are in Egypt, and have heard their cry because of their taskmasters, for I know their sorrows. So I have come down to deliver them out of the hand of the Egyptians, and to bring them up from that land to a good and large land, to a land flowing with milk and honey, to the place of the Canaanites and the Hittites and the Amorites and the Perizzites and the Hivites and the Jebusites. Now therefore, behold, the cry of the children of Israel has come to Me, and I have also seen the oppression with which the Egyptians oppress them. Come now, therefore, and I will send you to Pharaoh that you may bring My people, the children of Israel, out of Egypt."

—Exodus 3:7–10

Table
of
Contents

Part 1: Showdown
True God v. False Gods—Moses v. Pharaoh

Part 2: The Great Deliverance

Part 3: From the Exodus
Toward the Promised Land

Introduction

From the Publishers

Through four long centuries, God's people endured slavery in Egypt. Worked like animals, whipped and beaten, forbidden to worship their God—they sank into despair.

Then God said, "Enough."

He called a reluctant Moses to deliver His people at last. Through Moses, God would make the impossible possible.

So a time came when the true God and Moses confronted Egypt's false gods and its stubborn Pharaoh. Only one side could prevail in this contest. The Exodus is the epic story of the great deliverance—the time when God suddenly intervened and led His people out of Egypt and slavery and ultimately, to the Promised Land.

The Exodus is not a fairy tale or fable. It really happened—and archaeology and history confirm that it did. The primary record of this stunning story is found in the second book of the Bible, bearing the name of the great deliverance: Exodus.

In recent times, the storytellers of our age—authors and film-makers—have more than once attempted to bring the Exodus to us in books or visually in theaters worldwide. Some things about the story, they get right. But so often, they depart from the truth of the Bible, as if it were not already dramatic enough just as written. Whether intended or not, their efforts fall short, focusing far too much on the human and not at all enough on the divine. Screenwriters cast about for something to "explain" the miracles of that deliverance—as miracles, like all things supernatural, are viewed with undisguised skepticism.

But in this book, we recount the Exodus just as its leader—Moses—recorded it, preserved for all time in the Bible's Old Testament. The Exodus, when told faithfully, brings glory and honor to the one true God—and it shows the sad powerlessness of the many gods worshipped by Pharaoh and all Egyptians. What an awesome showdown! The true God versus an array of false gods; Moses versus Pharaoh.

A Story Recorded for Us but Also About Us!

Just reading this magnificent story—whether for a countless time or for the first time ever—is worth the time of any of us to invest. But this is not just an ancient tale to pique our imaginations or to entertain us with a barnburner of a good story.

The reason we share this story again here is because it speaks not only *to* us but *of* us! You see, the plagues that befell Egypt are to be repeated in the near future. The great deliverance of God's true people is also to be repeated. In the pages ahead, we will share just how and why, as well as when.

Another clear and personal lesson is ours to learn in this amazing story: Not only does God deliver His people as a nation or church or people—He also is available every new day to deliver us individually. He can deliver you, reading friend. And make no mistake about it: You, and everyone living and breathing on this planet—are enslaved. We are each and all slaves to a seemingly endless variety of sins. Despite our best efforts and intentions, we lie. We cheat. We steal. We commit adultery. We hurt others. We live selfish, pride-filled lives centered on advancing the wants and desires of Number One—ourselves. We give lip service to God and spiritual things but live as if He didn't exist. We're addicted to habits and behaviors from which we can't escape.

We Need Deliverance

Yes, we desperately need deliverance. And if we let Him, the same all-powerful God who parted the Red Sea for Israel and delivered them from the thundering pursuit of Pharaoh and his minions intent on slaughtering them—that same all-powerful God will deliver us too. He can deliver us from the strongest, most ingrained habits or addictions. He can totally, utterly, radically change us from the inside out. What we once loved, we'll now hate. What we once hated, we'll now love. That kind of change takes massive power to make happen. But the God of the Red Sea and the Exodus is the same—the very same—God who stands ready to deliver each of us from our strongest chains of sin.

So let this story of the Exodus bring you your own great deliverance. Let it bring you hope such as you've never experienced before. Let the ancient Exodus be proof to you that when you stand in life with the sea in front, mountains to the side, and the devil and his demons pursuing you, you are moments away from God's personal and dramatic deliverance.

In the pages just ahead, see just how powerful *your* God is!

The Author of This Book

E. G. White (1827–1915) wrote and lived among the most formidable vessels heaven has ever used in the not-too-distant past of church history. Christian luminaries such as Dwight L. Moody, F. B. Meyer, Henry Drummond, R. A. Torrey, Charles Spurgeon, and Oswald Chambers pushed the kingdom forward through scholarship, biblical preaching, and evangelistic endeavors.

E. G. White advanced the kingdom by pen. An extraordinary woman, her genteel manner lighted upon every work she produced, which made her revolutionary ideas palatable and accessible to the common soul while refreshing the theologian with her expression of simplicity. Her pen has stirred millions into a deeper knowledge of their Savior, a broader concept of education, a more meaningful approach to health, a revived appreciation of the power of the home, and to a style of leadership that values integrity supremely.

She wrote more than 5,000 periodical articles and 40 books during her lifetime. But today—including compilations from her 50,000 page of manuscripts—more than 120 titles are available in English. This is remarkable, considering the fact that her formal schooling ended at age 9!

E. G. White is the most translated female nonfiction writer in the entire history of literature and also the most translated American nonfiction author of either gender. Her life-changing masterpiece on Christian living, *Steps to Christ,* has been published in about 150 languages.

Her crowning literary achievement is the five-volume *Century Classics Collection.* Widely acclaimed as one of the best devotional commentaries on the entire Bible, the *Century Classics* begins and ends with the theme "God Is Love."

The contents of this present book on the Exodus are drawn from two of the principal works of E. G. White in the five-volume *E. G. White Century Classics Collection.* The books are *Patriarchs and Prophets* and *The Great Controversy.* In these works she has insightfully expounded upon the account of Moses and the Exodus, and their relation to our day and the end of time.

E. G. White lived most of her life during the nineteenth century, and as is characteristic of literary writers during that century, paragraphs and chapters tend to be long. In this present work—*EXODUS: The Great Deliverance*—the publishers have broken up long chapters and paragraphs, and where deemed necessary, have inserted subheadings and pull-out quotes in the text of E. G. White's original material. These editorial tweaks are designed to allow for easier reading for today's contemporary audience. But none of these minor editorial helps by the publishers have altered the original text of the books from which the present volume is excerpted.

The Message of the Book

As you move forward into this book, you'll discover that it is divided into three sections, each one advancing the story of the Exodus through time.

In **Part 1**, the author steps back in time to provide the background for the upcoming Exodus, first introducing God's chosen leader to accomplish this huge task: Moses. This section of the book shares the misery and oppression of God's people under Egyptian slavery. Then, with the Exodus imminent, this part of the book chronicles the ten great plagues God sent in a futile attempt to persuade hard-hearted Pharaoh—Egypt's leader—to let the Israelites go free. Part 1 then leaps through time from ancient Egypt to a time that is to us yet future—a time when again, God will send plagues upon those who oppose and even persecute His people.

Part 2 returns us to Egypt and details for us the Passover—God's sign placed on the dwelling of every faithful Israelite, indicating that when the destroying angel should come to do his work of justice, those followers of God would be "passed over"—spared from the destruction. The tenth and final plague was to be the death of every firstborn living in a dwelling not marked to be passed over.

Finally, the Pharaoh relents and lets God's people go, and this book's author records the story of how their journey to freedom began—only to be threatened when Pharaoh changed his mind and led his military in pursuit of them. Israel soon reached a place where they found themselves trapped—the Red Sea just ahead of them, mountains all around them, and Pharaoh's army closing in fast.

Then came the great deliverance! God parted the Red Sea, and His people walked through to the opposite side on a dry path. Once safely on the Sinai side of the Red Sea, the Egyptians thundered after them, using the same open path—only for it to suddenly close up again and drown them all.

At this point in Part 2, the author leaps ahead in time again to the future—to a time when once again, the fate of God's people appears hopeless. Yet once again, God delivers His people, and very soon, Jesus—God in human form—returns to Earth to save His followers and take them with Him to Heaven.

Part 3 of this book follows the journey of Israel from the Red Sea to Mount Sinai, on their way to the Promised Land. At Sinai, God gives them His law, which they had largely forgotten during their 400-year sojourn in Egypt. So far were they from the law that when Moses descended from Mount Sinai with tablets containing the law written by God's own fingers, the people had given themselves over to revelry and idol worship.

This book—*EXODUS: The Great Deliverance*—does not follow Israel's 40-year trek through the desert to the Promised Land. But the larger book from which this one is extracted carries that story forward, and we as publishers highly recommend you obtain your own copy of it, entitled *Patriarchs and Prophets*—or better yet, purchase the full *E. G. White Century Classics Collection*. You'll find ordering information at the end of this book.

Part 1

Showdown:
True God vs. False gods;
Moses vs. Pharaoh

Part 1

∞

Thought Questions

- In trying to stop an attack on a fellow Israelite, Moses killed the Egyptian attacker. Later, God told Moses that He had chosen him to deliver Israel from their captivity. Moses protested, but God said to him, "I will be with you." Do you believe that if God calls you to do something for Him—despite your past sins—He will also be with you?

- The Egyptians taunted the Israelites and said, "If your God had any power, why hasn't He made you a free people?" How can we keep on trusting God when it seems that we as His true followers are not doing nearly as well as those who mock Him, yet prosper?

- Before God delivered His people from Egyptian slavery, He sent judgments in the form of plagues upon Pharaoh and the Egyptians. At the very end of time—yet future—He will once again send plagues on the evil multitudes who persecute His people. But in both cases, God was setting the stage for deliverance. Do you have enough faith in God to trust Him to deliver His people, despite the threats of persecution?

Chapter 1

This chapter is based on Exodus 1–4.

God Raises Up a Leader

The people of Egypt, in order to supply themselves with food during the famine, had sold to the crown their cattle and lands, and had finally bound themselves to perpetual serfdom. Joseph wisely provided for their release; he permitted them to become royal tenants, holding their lands of the king, and paying an annual tribute of one fifth of the products of their labor.

But the children of Jacob were not under the necessity of making such conditions. On account of the service that Joseph had rendered the Egyptian nation, they were not only granted a part of the country as a home, but were exempted from taxation, and liberally supplied with food during the continuance of the famine. The king publicly acknowledged that it was through the merciful interposition of the God of Joseph that Egypt enjoyed plenty while other nations were perishing from famine. He saw, too, that Joseph's management had greatly enriched the kingdom, and his gratitude surrounded the family of Jacob with royal favor.

But as time rolled on, the great man to whom Egypt owed so much, and the generation blessed by his labors, passed to the grave. And "there arose up a new king over Egypt, which knew not Joseph." Not that he was ignorant of Joseph's services to the nation, but he wished to make no recognition of them, and, so far as possible, to bury them in oblivion. "And he said unto his people, Behold, the people of the children of Israel are more and mightier than we: come on, let us deal wisely with them; lest they multiply, and it come to pass, that, when there falleth out any war, they join also unto our enemies, and fight against us, and so get them up out of the land."

The Bitter Bondage of an Enslaved Nation

The Israelites had already become very numerous; they "were fruitful, and increased abundantly, and multiplied, and waxed exceeding mighty; and the land was filled with them." Under Joseph's fostering care, and the favor of the king who was then ruling, they had spread rapidly over the land. But they had kept themselves a distinct race, having nothing in common with the Egyptians in customs or religion; and their increasing numbers now excited the fears of the king and his people, lest in case of war they should join themselves with the enemies of Egypt. Yet policy forbade their banishment from the country. Many of them were able and understanding workmen, and they added greatly to the wealth of the nation; the king needed such laborers for the erection of his magnificent palaces and temples. Accordingly he ranked them with the Egyptians who had sold themselves with their possessions to the kingdom. Soon taskmasters were set over them, and their slavery became complete.

> *Taskmasters were set over them, and their slavery became complete.*
>
>

"And the Egyptians made the children of Israel to serve with rigor: and they made their lives bitter with hard bondage, in mortar, and in brick, and in all manner of service in the field: all their service, wherein they made them serve, was with rigor." "But the more they afflicted them, the more they multiplied and grew."

The king and his counselors had hoped to subdue the Israelites with hard labor, and thus decrease their numbers and crush out their independent spirit. Failing to accomplish their purpose, they proceeded to more cruel measures. Orders were issued to the women whose employment gave them opportunity for executing the command, to destroy the Hebrew male children at their birth. Satan was the mover in this matter. He knew that a deliverer was to be raised up among the Israelites; and by leading the king to destroy their children he hoped to defeat the divine purpose. But the women feared God, and dared not execute the cruel mandate. The Lord approved their course, and prospered them. The king, angry at the failure of his design, made the command more urgent and extensive. The whole nation was called upon to hunt out and slaughter his helpless victims. "And Pharaoh charged all his people, saying, Every son that is born ye shall cast into the river, and every daughter ye shall save alive."

While this decree was in full force a son was born to Amram and Jochebed, devout Israelites of the tribe of Levi. The babe was "a goodly child;" and the parents, believing that the time of Israel's release was drawing near, and that God would raise up a deliverer for His people, determined that their little one should not be sacrificed. Faith in God strengthened their hearts, "and they were not afraid of the king's commandment." Hebrews 11:23.

The mother succeeded in concealing the child for three months. Then, finding that she could no longer keep him safely, she prepared a little ark of rushes, making it watertight by means of slime and pitch; and laying the babe therein, she placed it among the flags at the river's brink. She dared not remain to guard it, lest the child's life and her own should be forfeited; but his sister, Miriam, lingered near, apparently indifferent, but anxiously watching to see what would become of her little brother. And there were other watchers. The mother's earnest prayers had committed her child to the care of God; and angels, unseen, hovered above his lowly resting place. Angels directed Pharaoh's daughter thither. Her curiosity was excited by the little basket, and as she looked upon the beautiful child within, she read the story at a glance. The tears of the babe awakened her compassion, and her sympathies went out to the unknown mother who had resorted to this means to preserve the life of her precious little one. She determined that he should be saved; she would adopt him as her own.

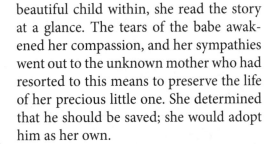

The mother's earnest prayers had committed her child to the care of God.

Miriam had been secretly noting every movement; perceiving that the child was tenderly regarded, she ventured nearer, and at last said, "Shall I go and call to thee a nurse of the Hebrew women, that she may nurse the child for thee?" And permission was given.

The sister hastened to her mother with the happy news, and without delay returned with her to the presence of Pharaoh's daughter. "Take this child away, and nurse it for me, and I will give thee thy wages," said the princess.

God had heard the mother's prayers; her faith had been rewarded. It was with deep gratitude that she entered upon her now safe and happy task. She faithfully improved her opportunity to educate her child for God. She felt confident that he had been preserved for some great work, and she knew that he must soon be given up to his royal mother, to be surrounded with influences that would tend to lead him away from God. All this rendered her more diligent and careful in his instruction than in that of her other children. She endeavored to imbue his mind with the fear of God and the love of truth and justice, and earnestly prayed that he might be preserved from every corrupting influence. She showed him the folly and sin of idolatry, and early taught him to bow down and pray to the living God, who alone could hear him and help him in every emergency.

She kept the boy as long as she could, but was obliged to give him up when he was about twelve years old. From his humble cabin home he was taken to the royal palace, to the daughter of Pharaoh, "and he became her son." Yet even here he did not lose the impressions received in childhood. The lessons learned at his mother's side could not be forgotten. They were a shield from the pride, the infidelity, and the vice that flourished amid the splendor of the court.

The Important Work of the Christian Mother

How far-reaching in its results was the influence of that one Hebrew woman, and she an exile and a slave! The whole future life of Moses, the great mission which he fulfilled as the leader of Israel, testifies to the importance of the work of the Christian mother. There is no other work that can equal this. To a very great extent the mother holds in her own hands the destiny of her children. She is dealing with developing minds and characters, working not alone for time, but for eternity. She is sowing seed that will spring up and bear fruit, either for good or for evil. She has not to paint a form of beauty upon canvas or to chisel it from marble, but to impress upon a human soul the image of the divine. Especially during their early years the responsibility rests upon her of forming the character of her children. The impressions now made upon their developing minds will remain with them all through life. Parents should direct the instruction and training of their children while very young, to the end that they may be Christians. They are placed in our care to be trained, not as heirs to the throne of an earthly empire, but as kings unto God, to reign through unending ages.

Let every mother feel that her moments are priceless; her work will be tested in the solemn day of accounts. Then it will be found that many of the failures and crimes of men and women have resulted from the ignorance and neglect of those whose duty it was to guide their childish feet in the right way. Then it will be found that many who have blessed the world with the light of genius and truth and holiness, owe the principles that were the mainspring of their influence and success to a praying, Christian mother.

Moses Trained to
Be Pharaoh's Successor

At the court of Pharaoh, Moses received the highest civil and military training. The monarch had determined to make his adopted grandson his successor on the throne, and the youth was educated for his high station. "And Moses was learned in all the wisdom of the Egyptians, and was mighty in words and in deeds." Acts 7:22. His ability as a military leader made him a favorite with the armies of Egypt, and he was generally regarded as a remarkable character. Satan had been defeated in his purpose. The very decree condemning the Hebrew children to death had been overruled by God for the training and education of the future leader of His people.

The elders of Israel were taught by angels that the time for their deliverance was near, and that Moses was the man whom God would employ to accomplish this work. Angels instructed Moses also that Jehovah had chosen him to break the bondage of His people. He, supposing that they were to obtain their freedom by force of arms, expected to lead the Hebrew host against the armies of Egypt, and having this in view, he guarded his affections, lest in his attachment to his foster mother or to Pharaoh he would not be free to do the will of God.

By the laws of Egypt all who occupied the throne of the Pharaohs must become members of the priestly caste; and Moses, as the heir apparent, was to be initiated into the mysteries of the national religion. This duty was committed to the priests. But while he was an ardent and untiring student, he could not be induced to participate in the worship of the gods. He was threatened with the loss of the crown, and warned that he would be disowned by the princess should he persist in his adherence to the Hebrew faith. But he was unshaken in his determination to render homage to none save the one God, the Maker of heaven and earth. He reasoned with priests and worshipers, showing the folly of their superstitious veneration of senseless objects. None could refute his arguments or change his purpose, yet for the time his firmness was tolerated on account of his high position and the favor with which he was regarded by both the king and the people.

As historian, poet, philosopher, general of armies, and legislator, Moses stands without a peer.

"By faith Moses, when he was come to years, refused to be called the son of Pharaoh's daughter; choosing rather to suffer affliction with the people of God, than to enjoy the pleasures of sin for a season; esteeming the reproach of Christ greater riches than the treasures in Egypt: for he had respect unto the recompense of the reward." Hebrews 11:24-26. Moses was fitted to take pre-eminence among the great of the earth, to shine in the courts of its most glorious kingdom, and to sway the scepter of its power. His intellectual greatness distinguishes him above the great men of all ages. As historian, poet, philosopher, general of armies, and legislator, he stands without a peer. Yet with the world before him, he had the moral strength to refuse the flattering prospects of wealth and greatness and fame, "choosing rather to suffer affliction with the people of God, than to enjoy the pleasures of sin for a season."

Moses had been instructed in regard to the final reward to be given to the humble and obedient servants of God, and worldly gain sank to its proper insignificance in comparison. The magnificent palace of Pharaoh and the monarch's throne were held out as an inducement to Moses; but he knew that the sinful pleasures that make men forget God were in its lordly courts. He looked beyond the gorgeous palace, beyond a monarch's crown, to the high honors that will be bestowed on the saints of the Most High in a kingdom untainted by sin. He saw by faith an imperishable crown that the King of heaven would place on the brow of the overcomer. This faith led him to turn away from the lordly ones of earth and join the humble, poor, despised nation that had chosen to obey God rather than to serve sin.

Moses Wrongly Assumes the Role of Avenger

Moses remained at court until he was forty years of age. His thoughts often turned upon the abject condition of his people, and he visited his brethren in their servitude, and encouraged them with the assurance that God would work for their deliverance. Often, stung to resentment by the sight of injustice and oppression, he burned to avenge their wrongs. One day, while thus abroad, seeing an Egyptian smiting an Israelite, he sprang forward and slew the Egyptian. Except the Israelite, there had been no witness to the deed, and Moses immediately buried the body in the sand. He had now shown himself ready to maintain the cause of his people, and he hoped to see them rise to recover their liberty. "He supposed his brethren would have understood how that God by his hand would deliver them; but they understood not." Acts 7:25. They were not yet prepared for freedom. On the following day Moses saw two Hebrews striving together, one of them evidently at fault. Moses reproved the offender, who at once retaliated upon the reprover, denying his right to interfere, and basely accusing him of crime: "Who made thee a prince and a judge over us?" he said. "Intendest thou to kill me, as thou killedst the Egyptian?"

The whole matter was quickly made known to the Egyptians, and, greatly exaggerated, soon reached the ears of Pharaoh. It was represented to the king that this act meant much; that Moses designed to lead his people against the Egyptians, to overthrow the government, and to seat himself upon the throne; and that there could be no security for the kingdom while he lived. It was at once determined by the monarch that he should die; but, becoming aware of his danger, he made his escape and fled toward Arabia.

The Lord directed his course, and he found a home with Jethro, the priest and prince of Midian, who was also a worshiper of God. After a time Moses married one of the daughters of Jethro; and here, in the service of his father-in-law, as keeper of his flocks, he remained forty years.

In slaying the Egyptian, Moses had fallen into the same error so often committed by his fathers, of taking into their own hands the work that God had promised to do. It was not God's will to deliver His people by warfare, as Moses thought, but by His own mighty power, that the glory might be ascribed to Him alone. Yet even this rash act was overruled by God to accomplish His purposes. Moses was not prepared for his great work. He had yet to learn the same lesson of faith that Abraham and Jacob had been taught—not to rely upon human strength or wisdom, but upon the power of God for the fulfillment of His promises. And there were other lessons that, amid the solitude of the mountains, Moses was to receive. In the school of self-denial and hardship he was to learn patience, to temper his passions. Before he could govern wisely, he must be trained to obey. His own heart must be fully in harmony with God before he could teach the knowledge of His will to Israel. By his own experience he must be prepared to exercise a fatherly care over all who needed his help.

> *In the school of self-denial and hardship Moses was to learn patience.*
>
>

Man would have dispensed with that long period of toil and obscurity, deeming it a great loss of time. But Infinite Wisdom called him who was to become the leader of his people to spend forty years in the humble work of a shepherd. The habits of caretaking, of self-forgetfulness and tender solicitude for his flock, thus developed, would prepare him to become the compassionate, longsuffering shepherd of Israel. No advantage that human training or culture could bestow, could be a substitute for this experience.

Moses had been learning much that he must unlearn. The influences that had surrounded him in Egypt—the love of his foster mother, his own high position as the king's grandson, the dissipation on every hand, the refinement, the subtlety, and the mysticism of a false religion, the splendor of idolatrous worship, the solemn grandeur of architecture and sculpture—all had left deep impressions upon his developing mind and had molded, to some extent, his habits and character. Time, change of surroundings, and communion with God could remove these impressions. It would require on the part of Moses himself a struggle as for life to renounce error and accept truth, but God would be his helper when the conflict should be too severe for human strength.

In all who have been chosen to accomplish a work for God the human element is seen. Yet they have not been men of stereotyped habits and character, who were satisfied to remain in that condition.

They earnestly desired to obtain wisdom from God and to learn to work for Him. Says the apostle, "If any of you lack wisdom, let him ask of God, that giveth to all men liberally, and upbraideth not; and it shall be given him." James 1:5. But God will not impart to men divine light while they are content to remain in darkness. In order to receive God's help, man must realize his weakness and deficiency; he must apply his own mind to the great change to be wrought in himself; he must be aroused to earnest and persevering prayer and effort. Wrong habits and customs must be shaken off; and it is only by determined endeavor to correct these errors and to conform to right principles that the victory can be gained. Many never attain to the position that they might occupy, because they wait for God to do for them that which He has given them power to do for themselves. All who are fitted for usefulness must be trained by the severest mental and moral discipline, and God will assist them by uniting divine power with human effort.

In the stern simplicity of his wilderness life, the results of the ease and luxury of Egypt disappeared.

Shut in by the bulwarks of the mountains, Moses was alone with God. The magnificent temples of Egypt no longer impressed his mind with their superstition and falsehood. In the solemn grandeur of the everlasting hills he beheld the majesty of the Most High, and in contrast realized how powerless and insignificant were the gods of Egypt. Everywhere the Creator's name was written. Moses seemed to stand in His presence and to be over-shadowed by His power. Here his pride and self-sufficiency were swept away. In the stern simplicity of his wilderness life, the results of the ease and luxury of Egypt disappeared. Moses became patient, reverent, and humble, "very meek, above all the men which were upon the face of the earth" (Numbers 12:3), yet strong in faith in the mighty God of Jacob.

As the years rolled on, and he wandered with his flocks in solitary places, pondering upon the oppressed condition of his people, he recounted the dealings of God with his fathers and the promises that were the heritage of the chosen nation, and his prayers for Israel ascended by day and by night. Heavenly angels shed their light around him. Here, under the inspiration of the Holy Spirit, he wrote the book of Genesis. The long years spent amid the desert solitudes were rich in blessing, not alone to Moses and his people, but to the world in all succeeding ages.

"And it came to pass in process of time, that the king of Egypt died: and the children of Israel sighed by reason of the bondage, and they cried, and their cry came up unto God by reason of the bondage. And God heard their groaning, and God remembered His covenant with Abraham, with Isaac, and with Jacob. And God looked upon the children of Israel, and God had respect unto them." The time for Israel's deliverance had come. But God's purpose was to be accomplished in a manner to pour contempt on human pride. The deliverer was to go forth as a humble shepherd, with only a rod in his hand; but God would make that rod the symbol of His power. Leading his flocks one day near Horeb, "the mountain of God," Moses saw a bush in flames, branches, foliage, and trunk, all burning, yet seeming not to be consumed. He drew near to view the wonderful sight, when a voice from out of the flame called him by name. With trembling lips he answered, "Here am I." He was warned not to approach irreverently: "Put off thy shoes from off thy feet; for the place whereon thou standest is holy ground. ... I am the God of thy father, the God of Abraham, the God of Isaac, and the God of Jacob." It was He who, as the Angel of the covenant, had revealed Himself to the fathers in ages past. "And Moses hid his face; for he was afraid to look upon God."

Approaching God With Reverence

Humility and reverence should characterize the deportment of all who come into the presence of God. In the name of Jesus we may come before Him with confidence, but we must not approach Him with the boldness of presumption, as though He were on a level with ourselves. There are those who address the great and all-powerful and holy God, who dwelleth in light unapproachable, as they would address an equal, or even an inferior. There are those who conduct themselves in His house as they would not presume to do in the audience chamber of an earthly ruler. These should remember that they are in His sight whom seraphim adore, before whom angels veil their faces. God is greatly to be reverenced; all who truly realize His presence will bow in humility before Him, and, like Jacob beholding the vision of God, they will cry out, "How dreadful is this place! This is none other but the house of God, and this is the gate of heaven."

The Assignment of the Great "I AM"

As Moses waited in reverent awe before God the words continued: "I have surely seen the affliction of My people which are in Egypt, and have heard their cry by reason of their taskmasters; for I know their sorrows; and I am come down to deliver them out of the hand of the Egyptians, and to bring them up out of that land unto a good land and a large, unto a land flowing with milk and honey. ... Come now therefore, and I will send thee unto Pharaoh, that thou mayest bring forth My people the children of Israel out of Egypt."

Amazed and terrified at the command, Moses drew back, saying, "Who am I, that I should go unto Pharaoh, and that I should bring forth the children of Israel out of Egypt?" The reply was, "Certainly I will be with thee; and this shall be a token unto thee, that I have sent thee: When thou hast brought forth the people out of Egypt, ye shall serve God upon this mountain."

Moses thought of the difficulties to be encountered, of the blindness, ignorance, and unbelief of his people, many of whom were almost destitute of a knowledge of God. "Behold," he said, "when I come unto the children of Israel, and shall say unto them, The God of your fathers hath sent me unto you; and they shall say to me, What is His name? what shall I say unto them?" The answer was—

I AM THAT I AM. Thus shalt thou say unto the children of Israel, I AM hath sent me unto you.

Moses was commanded first to assemble the elders of Israel, the most noble and righteous among them, who had long grieved because of their bondage, and to declare to them a message from God, with a promise of deliverance. Then he was to go with the elders before the king, and say to him—

The Lord God of the Hebrews hath met with us: and now let us go, we beseech thee, three days' journey into the wilderness, that we may sacrifice to the Lord our God.

Moses was forewarned that Pharaoh would resist the appeal to let Israel go. Yet the courage of God's servant must not fail; for the Lord would make this the occasion to manifest His power before the Egyptians and before His people. "And I will stretch out My hand, and smite Egypt with all My wonders which I will do in the midst thereof: and after that he will let you go."

Direction was also given concerning the provision they were to make for the journey. The Lord declared, "It shall come to pass, that, when ye go, ye shall not go empty: but every woman shall borrow of her neighbor, and of her that sojourneth in her house, jewels of silver, and jewels of gold, and raiment." The Egyptians had been enriched by the labor unjustly exacted from the Israelites, and as the latter were to start on the journey to their new home, it was right for them to claim the reward of their years of toil. They were to ask for articles of value, such as could be easily transported, and God would give them favor in the sight of the Egyptians. The mighty miracles wrought for their deliverance would strike terror to the oppressors, so that the requests of the bondmen would be granted.

Evidence That God Had Sent Moses

Moses saw before him difficulties that seemed insurmountable. What proof could he give his people that God had indeed sent him? "Behold," he said, "they will not believe me, nor hearken unto my voice: for they will say, The Lord hath not appeared unto thee." Evidence that appealed to his own senses was now given. He was told to cast his rod upon the ground. As he did so, "it became a serpent; and Moses fled from before it." He was commanded to seize it, and in his hand it became a rod. He was bidden to put his hand into his bosom. He obeyed, and "when he took it out, behold, his hand was leprous as snow." Being told to put it again into his bosom, he found on withdrawing it that it had become like the other. By these signs the Lord assured Moses that His own people, as well as Pharaoh, should be convinced that One mightier than the king of Egypt was manifest among them.

But the servant of God was still overwhelmed by the thought of the strange and wonderful work before him. In his distress and fear he now pleaded as an excuse a lack of ready speech: "O my Lord, I am not eloquent, neither heretofore, nor since Thou hast spoken unto Thy servant; but I am slow of speech, and of a slow tongue." He had been so long away from the Egyptians that he had not so clear knowledge and ready use of their language as when he was among them.

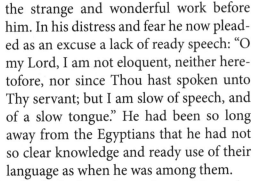

"I will be with thy mouth," God said, "and teach thee what thou shalt say.

The Lord said unto him, "Who hath made man's mouth? or who maketh the dumb, or deaf, or the seeing, or the blind? have not I the Lord?" To this was added another assurance of divine aid: "Now therefore go, and I will be with thy mouth, and teach thee what thou shalt say." But Moses still entreated that a more competent person be selected. These excuses at first proceeded from humility and diffidence; but after the Lord had promised to remove all difficulties, and to give him final success, then any further shrinking back and complaining of his unfitness showed distrust of God. It implied a fear that God was unable to qualify him for the great work to which He had called him, or that He had made a mistake in the selection of the man.

Moses was now directed to Aaron, his elder brother, who, having been in daily use of the language of the Egyptians, was able to speak it perfectly. He was told that Aaron was coming to meet him. The next words from the Lord were an unqualified command:

"Thou shalt speak unto him, and put words in his mouth: and I will be with thy mouth, and with his mouth, and will teach you what ye shall do. And he shall be thy spokesman unto the people: and he shall be, even he shall be to thee instead of a mouth, and thou shalt be to him instead of God. And thou shalt take this rod in thine hand, wherewith thou shalt do signs." He could make no further resistance, for all ground for excuse was removed.

The divine command given to Moses found him self-distrustful, slow of speech, and timid. He was overwhelmed with a sense of his incapacity to be a mouthpiece for God to Israel. But having once accepted the work, he entered upon it with his whole heart, putting all his trust in the Lord. The greatness of his mission called into exercise the best powers of his mind. God blessed his ready obedience, and he became eloquent, hopeful, self-possessed, and well fitted for the greatest work ever given to man. This is an example of what God does to strengthen the character of those who trust Him fully and give themselves unreservedly to His commands.

A man will gain power and efficiency as he accepts the responsibilities that God places upon him, and with his whole soul seeks to qualify himself to bear them aright. However humble his position or limited his ability, that man will attain true greatness who, trusting to divine strength, seeks to perform his work with fidelity. Had Moses relied upon his own strength and wisdom, and eagerly accepted the great charge, he would have evinced his entire unfitness for such a work. The fact that a man feels his weakness is at least some evidence that he realizes the magnitude of the work appointed him, and that he will make God his counselor and his strength.

That man will attain true greatness who seeks to perform his work with fidelity.

Moses returned to his father-in-law and expressed his desire to visit his brethren in Egypt. Jethro's consent was given, with his blessing, "Go in peace." With his wife and children, Moses set forth on the journey. He had not dared to make known the object of his mission, lest they should not be allowed to accompany him. Before reaching Egypt, however, he himself thought it best for their own safety to send them back to the home in Midian.

A secret dread of Pharaoh and the Egyptians, whose anger had been kindled against him forty years before, had rendered Moses still more reluctant to return to Egypt; but after he had set out to obey the divine command, the Lord revealed to him that his enemies were dead.

On the way from Midian, Moses received a startling and terrible warning of the Lord's displeasure. An angel appeared to him in a threatening manner, as if he would immediately destroy him. No explanation was given; but Moses remembered that he had disregarded one of God's requirements; yielding to the persuasion of his wife, he had neglected to perform the rite of circumcision upon their youngest son. He had failed to comply with the condition by which his child could be entitled to the blessings of God's covenant with Israel; and such a neglect on the part of their chosen leader could not but lessen the force of the divine precepts upon the people. Zipporah, fearing that her husband would be slain, performed the rite herself, and the angel then permitted Moses to pursue his journey. In his mission to Pharaoh, Moses was to be placed in a position of great peril; his life could be preserved only through the protection of holy angels. But while living in neglect of a known duty, he would not be secure; for he could not be shielded by the angels of God.

In the time of trouble just before the coming of Christ, the righteous will be preserved through the ministration of heavenly angels; but there will be no security for the transgressor of God's law. Angels cannot then protect those who are disregarding one of the divine precepts.

Chapter 2

This chapter is based on Exodus 5–10.

The Plagues Fall on Egypt

Aaron, being instructed by angels, went forth to meet his brother, from whom he had been so long separated; and they met amid the desert solitudes, near Horeb. Here they communed together, and Moses told Aaron "all the words of the Lord who had sent him, and all the signs which He had commanded him." Exodus 4:28. Together they journeyed to Egypt; and having reached the land of Goshen, they proceeded to assemble the elders of Israel. Aaron repeated to them all the dealings of God with Moses, and then the signs which God had given Moses were shown before the people. "The people believed: and when they heard that the Lord had visited the children of Israel, and that He had looked upon their affliction, then they bowed their heads and worshiped." Verse 31.

Moses had been charged also with a message for the king. The two brothers entered the palace of the Pharaohs as ambassadors from the King of kings, and they spoke in His name: "Thus saith Jehovah, God of Israel, Let My people go, that they may hold a feast unto Me in the wilderness."

"Who is Jehovah, that I should obey His voice to let Israel go?" demanded the monarch; "I know not Jehovah, neither will I let Israel go."

Their answer was, "The God of the Hebrews hath met with us: let us go, we pray thee, three days' journey into the desert, and sacrifice unto the Lord our God; lest He fall upon us with pestilence, or with the sword."

Tidings of them and of the interest they were exciting among the people had already reached the king. His anger was kindled. "Wherefore do ye, Moses and Aaron, let [hinder] the people from their works?" he said. "Get you unto your burdens." Already the kingdom had suffered loss by the interference of these strangers. At thought of this he added, "Behold, the people of the land now are many, and ye make them rest from their burdens."

In their bondage the Israelites had to some extent lost the knowledge of God's law, and they had departed from its precepts. The Sabbath had been generally disregarded, and the exactions of their taskmasters made its observance apparently impossible. But Moses had shown his people that obedience to God was the first condition of deliverance; and the efforts made to restore the observance of the Sabbath had come to the notice of their oppressors.

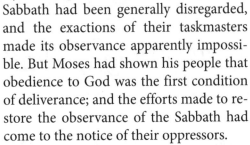

Moses had shown his people that obedience to God was the first condition of deliverance.

The king, thoroughly roused, suspected the Israelites of a design to revolt from his service. Disaffection was the result of idleness; he would see that no time was left them for dangerous scheming. And he at once adopted measures to tighten their bonds and crush out their independent spirit. The same day orders were issued that rendered their labor still more cruel and oppressive. The most common building material of that country was sun-dried brick; the walls of the finest edifices were made of this, and then faced with stone; and the manufacture of brick employed great numbers of the bondmen. Cut straw being intermixed with the clay, to hold it together, large quantities of straw were required for the work; the king now directed that no more straw be furnished; the laborers must find it for themselves, while the same amount of brick should be exacted.

This order produced great distress among the Israelites throughout the land. The Egyptian taskmasters had appointed Hebrew officers to oversee the work of the people, and these officers were responsible for the labor performed by those under their charge. When the requirement of the king was put in force, the people scattered themselves throughout the land, to gather stubble instead of straw; but they found it impossible to accomplish the usual amount of labor. For this failure the Hebrew officers were cruelly beaten.

These officers supposed that their oppression came from their taskmasters, and not from the king himself; and they went to him with their grievances. Their remonstrance was met by Pharaoh with a taunt: "Ye are idle, ye are idle: therefore ye say, Let us go and do sacrifice to the Lord." They were ordered back to their work, with the declaration that their burdens were in no case to be lightened.

Returning, they met Moses and Aaron, and cried out to them, "The Lord look upon you, and judge; because ye have made our savor to be abhorred in the eyes of Pharaoh, and in the eyes of his servants, to put a sword in their hand to slay us."

Moses' Distress for the Suffering of Israel

As Moses listened to these reproaches he was greatly distressed. The sufferings of the people had been much increased. All over the land a cry of despair went up from old and young, and all united in charging upon him the disastrous change in their condition. In bitterness of soul he went before God, with the cry, "Lord, wherefore hast Thou so evil entreated this people? why is it that Thou hast sent me? For since I came to Pharaoh to speak in Thy name, he hath done evil to this people; neither hast Thou delivered Thy people at all." The answer was, "Now shalt thou see what I will do to Pharaoh: for with a strong hand shall he let them go, and with a strong hand shall he drive them out of his land." Again he was pointed back to the covenant which God had made with the fathers, and was assured that it would be fulfilled.

During all the years of servitude in Egypt there had been among the Israelites some who adhered to the worship of Jehovah. These were solely troubled as they saw their children daily witnessing the abominations of the heathen, and even bowing down to their false gods. In their distress they cried unto the Lord for deliverance from the Egyptian yoke, that they might be freed from the corrupting influence of idolatry. They did not conceal their faith, but declared to the Egyptians that the object of their worship was the Maker of heaven and earth, the only true and living God. They rehearsed the evidences of His existence and power, from creation down to the days of Jacob. The Egyptians thus had an opportunity to become acquainted with the religion of the Hebrews; but disdaining to be instructed by their slaves, they tried to seduce the worshipers of God by promises of reward, and, this failing, by threats and cruelty.

They rehearsed the evidences of God's existence and power, from creation down to the days of Jacob.

The elders of Israel endeavored to sustain the sinking faith of their brethren by repeating the promises made to their fathers, and the prophetic words of Joseph before his death, foretelling their deliverance from Egypt. Some would listen and believe. Others, looking at the circumstances that surrounded them, refused to hope. The Egyptians, being informed of what was reported among their bondmen, derided their expectations and scornfully denied the power of their God. They pointed to their situation as a nation of slaves, and tauntingly said, "If your God is just and merciful, and possesses power above that of the Egyptian gods, why does He not make you a free people?" They called attention to their own condition. They worshiped deities termed by the Israelites false gods, yet they were a rich and powerful nation. They declared that their gods had blessed them with prosperity, and had given them the Israelites as servants, and they gloried in their power to oppress and destroy the worshipers of Jehovah. Pharaoh himself boasted that the God of the Hebrews could not deliver them from his hand.

Words like these destroyed the hopes of many of the Israelites. The case appeared to them very much as the Egyptians had represented. It was true that they were slaves, and must endure whatever their cruel taskmasters might choose to inflict. Their children had been hunted and slain, and their own lives were a burden. Yet they were worshiping the God of heaven. If Jehovah were indeed above all gods, surely He would not thus leave them in bondage to idolaters. But those who were true to God understood that it was because of Israel's departure from Him—because of their disposition to marry with heathen nations, thus being led into idolatry—that the Lord had permitted them to become bondmen; and they confidently assured their brethren that He would soon break the yoke of the oppressor.

The Hebrews had expected to obtain their freedom without any special trial of their faith or any real suffering or hardship. But they were not yet prepared for deliverance. They had little faith in God, and were unwilling patiently to endure their afflictions until He should see fit to work for them. Many were content to remain in bondage rather than meet the difficulties attending removal to a strange land; and the habits of some had become so much like those of the Egyptians that they preferred to dwell in Egypt. Therefore the Lord did not deliver them by the first manifestation of His power before Pharaoh. He overruled events more fully to develop the tyrannical spirit of the

Egyptian king and also to reveal Himself to His people. Beholding His justice, His power, and His love, they would choose to leave Egypt and give themselves to His service. The task of Moses would have been much less difficult had not many of the Israelites become so corrupted that they were unwilling to leave Egypt.

Moses went as he was commanded; but they would not listen.

The Lord directed Moses to go again to the people and repeat the promise of deliverance, with a fresh assurance of divine favor. He went as he was commanded; but they would not listen. Says the Scripture, "They hearkened not … for anguish of spirit, and for cruel bondage." Again the divine message came to Moses, "Go in, speak unto Pharaoh king of Egypt, that he let the children of Israel go out of his land." In discouragement he replied, "Behold, the children of Israel have not hearkened unto me; how then shall Pharaoh hear me?" He was told to take Aaron with him and go before Pharaoh, and again demand "that he send the children of Israel out of his land."

He was informed that the monarch would not yield until God should visit judgments upon Egypt and bring out Israel by the signal manifestation of His power. Before the infliction of each plague, Moses was to describe its nature and effects, that the king might save himself from it if he chose. Every punishment rejected would be followed by one more severe, until his proud heart would be humbled, and he would acknowledge the Maker of heaven and earth as the true and living God. The Lord would give the Egyptians an opportunity to see how vain was the wisdom of their mighty men, how feeble the power of their gods, when opposed to the commands of Jehovah. He would punish the people of Egypt for their idolatry and silence their boasting of the blessings received from their senseless deities. God would glorify His own name, that other nations might hear of His power and tremble at His mighty acts, and that His people might be led to turn from their idolatry and render Him pure worship.

The Rod Becomes a Serpent

Again Moses and Aaron entered the lordly halls of the king of Egypt. There, surrounded by lofty columns and glittering adornments, by the rich paintings and sculptured images of heathen gods, before the monarch of the most powerful kingdom then in existence, stood the two representatives of the enslaved race, to repeat the command from God for Israel's release. The king demanded a miracle, in evidence of their divine commission. Moses and Aaron had been directed how to act in case such a demand should be made, and Aaron now took the rod and cast it down before Pharaoh. It became a serpent. The monarch sent for his "wise men and the sorcerers," who "cast down every man his rod and they became serpents: but Aaron's rod swallowed up their rods." Then the king, more determined than before, declared his magicians equal in power with Moses and Aaron; he denounced the servants of the Lord as impostors, and felt himself secure in resisting their demands. Yet while he despised their message, he was restrained by divine power from doing them harm.

It was the hand of God, and no human influence or power possessed by Moses and Aaron, that wrought the miracles which they showed before Pharaoh. Those signs and wonders were designed to convince Pharaoh that the great "I AM" had sent Moses, and that it was the duty of the king to let Israel go, that they might serve the living God. The magicians also showed signs and wonders; for they wrought not by their own skill alone, but by the power of their god, Satan, who assisted them in counterfeiting the work of Jehovah.

> *Pharaoh desired to justify his stubbornness in resisting the divine command.*
>
>

The magicians did not really cause their rods to become serpents; but by magic, aided by the great deceiver, they were able to produce this appearance. It was beyond the power of Satan to change the rods to living serpents. The prince of evil, though possessing all the wisdom and might of an angel fallen, has not power to create, or to give life; this is the prerogative of God alone. But all that was in Satan's power to do, he did; he produced a counterfeit. To human sight the rods were changed to serpents. Such they were believed to be by Pharaoh and his court. There was nothing in their appearance to distinguish them from the serpent produced by Moses. Though the Lord caused the real serpent to swallow up the spurious ones, yet even this was regarded by Pharaoh, not as a work of God's power, but as the result of a kind of magic superior to that of his servants.

Pharaoh desired to justify his stubbornness in resisting the divine command, and hence he was seeking some pretext for disregarding the miracles that God had wrought through Moses. Satan gave him just what he wanted. By the work that he wrought through the magicians he made it appear to the Egyptians that Moses and Aaron were only magicians and sorcerers, and that the message they brought could not claim respect as coming from a superior being. Thus Satan's counterfeit accomplished its purpose of emboldening the Egyptians in their rebellion and causing Pharaoh to harden his heart against conviction. Satan hoped also to shake the faith of Moses and Aaron in the divine origin of their mission, that his instruments might prevail. He was unwilling that the children of Israel should be released from bondage to serve the living God.

But the prince of evil had a still deeper object in manifesting his wonders through the magicians. He well knew that Moses, in breaking the yoke of bondage from off the children of Israel, pre-figured Christ, who was to break the reign of sin over the human family. He knew that when Christ should appear, mighty miracles would be wrought as an evidence to the world that

> *Satan is constantly seeking to counterfeit the work of Christ.*

God had sent Him. Satan trembled for his power. By counterfeiting the work of God through Moses, he hoped not only to prevent the deliverance of Israel, but to exert an influence through future ages to destroy faith in the miracles of Christ. Satan is constantly seeking to counterfeit the work of Christ and to establish his own power and claims. He leads men to account for the miracles of Christ by making them appear to be the result of human skill and power. In many minds he thus destroys faith in Christ as the Son of God, and leads them to reject the gracious offers of mercy through the plan of redemption.

Moses and Aaron were directed to visit the riverside next morning, where the king was accustomed to repair. The overflowing of the Nile being the source of food and wealth for all Egypt, the river was worshiped as a god, and the monarch came thither daily to pay his devotions. Here the two brothers again repeated the message to him, and then they stretched out the rod and smote upon the water. The sacred stream ran blood, the fish died, and the river became offensive to the smell. The water in the houses, the supply preserved in cisterns, was likewise changed to blood. But "the magicians of Egypt did so with their enchantments," and "Pharaoh turned and went into his house, neither did he set his heart to this also." For seven days the plague continued, but without effect.

Again the rod was stretched out over the waters, and frogs came up from the river and spread over the land. They overran the houses, took possession of the bed chambers, and even the ovens and kneading troughs. The frog was regarded as sacred by the Egyptians, and they would not destroy it; but the slimy pests had now become intolerable. They swarmed even in the palace of the Pharaohs, and the king was impatient to have them removed. The magicians had appeared to produce frogs, but they could not remove them. Upon seeing this, Pharaoh was somewhat humbled. He sent for Moses and Aaron, and said, "Entreat the Lord, that He may take away the frogs from me, and from my people; and I will let the people go, that they may do sacrifice unto the Lord." After reminding the king of his former boasting, they requested him to appoint a time when they should pray for the removal of the plague. He set the next day, secretly hoping that in the interval the frogs might disappear of themselves, and thus save him from the bitter humiliation of submitting to the God of Israel. The plague, however, continued till the time specified, when throughout all Egypt the frogs died, but their putrid bodies, which remained, polluted the atmosphere.

Appeal and warning were ineffectual, and another judgment was inflicted.

The Lord could have caused them to return to dust in a moment; but He did not do this lest after their removal the king and his people should pronounce it the result of sorcery or enchantment, like the work of the magicians. The frogs died, and were then gathered together in heaps. Here the king and all Egypt had evidence which their vain philosophy could not gainsay, that this work was not accomplished by magic, but was a judgment from the God of heaven.

"When Pharaoh saw that there was respite, he hardened his heart." At the command of God, Aaron stretched out his hand, and the dust of the earth became lice throughout all the land of Egypt. Pharaoh called upon the magicians to do the same, but they could not. The work of God was thus shown to be superior to that of Satan.

The magicians themselves acknowledged, "This is the finger of God." But the king was still unmoved.

Appeal and warning were ineffectual, and another judgment was inflicted. The time of its occurrence was foretold, that it might not be said to have come by chance. Flies filled the houses and swarmed upon the ground, so that "the land was corrupted by reason of the swarms of flies." These flies were large and venomous, and their bite was extremely painful to man and beast. As had been foretold, this visitation did not extend to the land of Goshen.

Pharaoh now offered the Israelites permission to sacrifice in Egypt, but they refused to accept such conditions. "It is not meet," said Moses; "lo, shall we sacrifice the abomination of the Egyptians before their eyes, and will they not stone us?" The animals which the Hebrews would be required to sacrifice were among those regarded as sacred by the Egyptians; and such was the reverence in which these creatures were held, that to slay one, even accidentally, was a crime punishable with death. It would be impossible for the Hebrews to worship in Egypt without giving offense to their masters. Moses again proposed to go three days' journey into the wilderness. The monarch consented, and begged the servants of God to entreat that the plague might be removed. They promised to do this, but warned him against dealing deceitfully with them. The plague was stayed, but the king's heart had become hardened by persistent rebellion, and he still refused to yield.

The king's heart had become hardened by persistent rebellion, and he still refused to yield.

A more terrible stroke followed—murrain upon all the Egyptian cattle that were in the field. Both the sacred animals and the beasts of burden—kine and oxen and sheep, horses and camels and asses—were destroyed. It had been distinctly stated that the Hebrews were to be exempt; and Pharaoh, on sending messengers to the home of the Israelites, proved the truth of this declaration of Moses. "Of the cattle of the children of Israel died not one." Still the king was obstinate.

Moses was next directed to take ashes of the furnace, and "sprinkle it toward heaven in the sight of Pharaoh." This act was deeply significant. Four hundred years before, God had shown to Abraham the future oppression of His people, under the figure of a smoking furnace and a burning lamp. He had declared that He would visit judgments upon their oppressors, and would bring forth the captives with great substance. In Egypt, Israel had long languished in the furnace of affliction. This act of Moses was an assurance to them that God was mindful of His covenant, and that the time for their deliverance had come.

As the ashes were sprinkled toward heaven, the fine particles spread over all the land of Egypt, and wherever they settled, produced boils "breaking forth with blains upon man, and upon beast." The priests and magicians had hitherto encouraged Pharaoh in his stubbornness, but now a judgment had come that reached even them. Smitten with a loathsome and painful disease, their vaunted power only making them contemptible, they were no longer able to contend against the God of Israel. The whole nation was made to see the folly of trusting in the magicians, when they were not able to protect even their own persons.

Still the heart of Pharaoh grew harder. And now the Lord sent a message to him, declaring, "I will at this time send all My plagues upon thy heart, and upon thy servants, and upon thy people; that thou mayest know that there is none like Me in all the earth. ... And in very deed for this cause have I raised thee up, for to show in thee My power." Not that God had given him an existence for this purpose, but His providence had overruled events to place him upon the throne at the very time appointed for Israel's deliverance. Though this haughty tyrant had by his crimes forfeited the mercy of God, yet his life had been preserved that through his stubbornness the Lord might manifest His wonders in the land of Egypt. The disposing of events is of God's providence. He could have placed upon the throne a more merciful king, who would not have dared to withstand the mighty manifestations of divine power. But in that case the Lord's purposes would not have been accomplished. His people were permitted to experience the grinding cruelty of the Egyptians, that they might not be deceived concerning the debasing influence of idolatry. In His dealing with Pharaoh, the Lord manifested His hatred of idolatry and His determination to punish cruelty and oppression.

Who Really Hardened Pharaoh's Heart?

God had declared concerning Pharaoh, "I will harden his heart, that he shall not let the people go." Exodus 4:21. There was no exercise of supernatural power to harden the heart of the king. God gave to Pharaoh the most striking evidence of divine power, but the monarch stubbornly refused to heed the light. Every display of infinite power rejected by him, rendered him the more determined in his rebellion. The seeds of rebellion that he sowed when he rejected the first miracle, produced their harvest. As he continued to venture on in his own course, going from one degree of stubbornness to another, his heart became more and more hardened, until he was called to look upon the cold, dead faces of the first-born.

God speaks to men through His servants, giving cautions and warnings, and rebuking sin. He gives to each an opportunity to correct his errors before they become fixed in the character; but if one refuses to be corrected, divine power does not interpose to counteract the tendency of his own action. He finds it more easy to repeat the same course. He is hardening the heart against the influence of the Holy Spirit. A further rejection of light places him where a far stronger influence will be ineffectual to make an abiding impression.

He who has once yielded to temptation will yield more readily the second time. Every repetition of the sin lessens his power of resistance, blinds his eyes, and stifles conviction. Every seed of indulgence sown will bear fruit. God works no miracle to prevent the harvest. "Whatsoever a man soweth, that shall he also reap." Galatians 6:7. He who manifests an infidel hardihood, a stolid indifference to divine truth, is but reaping the harvest of that which he has himself sown. It is thus that multitudes come to listen with stoical indifference to the truths that once stirred their very souls. They sowed neglect and resistance to the truth, and such is the harvest which they reap.

> *He who has once yielded to temptation will yield more readily the second time.*
>
>

Those who are quieting a guilty conscience with the thought that they can change a course of evil when they choose, that they can trifle with the invitations of mercy, and yet be again and again impressed, take this course at their peril. They think that after casting all their influence on the side of the great rebel, in a moment of utmost extremity, when danger compasses them about, they will change leaders. But this is not so easily done. The experience, the education, the discipline of a life of sinful indulgence, has so thoroughly molded the character that they cannot then receive the image of Jesus. Had no light shone upon their pathway, the case would have been different. Mercy might interpose, and give them an opportunity to accept her overtures; but after light has been long rejected and despised, it will be finally withdrawn.

The contest was not ended. Pharaoh's confessions and promises were not the effect of any radical change.

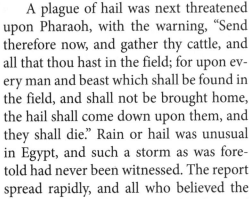

A plague of hail was next threatened upon Pharaoh, with the warning, "Send therefore now, and gather thy cattle, and all that thou hast in the field; for upon every man and beast which shall be found in the field, and shall not be brought home, the hail shall come down upon them, and they shall die." Rain or hail was unusual in Egypt, and such a storm as was foretold had never been witnessed. The report spread rapidly, and all who believed the word of the Lord gathered in their cattle, while those who despised the warning left them in the field. Thus in the midst of judgment the mercy of God was displayed, the people were tested, and it was shown how many had been led to fear God by the manifestation of His power.

The storm came as predicted—thunder and hail, and fire mingled with it, "very grievous, such as there was none like it in all the land of Egypt since it became a nation. And the hail smote throughout all the land of Egypt all that was in the field, both man and beast; and the hail smote every herb of the field, and brake every tree of the field." Ruin and desolation marked the path of the destroying angel. The land of Goshen alone was spared. It was demonstrated to the Egyptians that the earth is under the control of the living God, that the elements obey His voice, and that the only safety is in obedience to Him.

All Egypt trembled before the awful outpouring of divine judgment. Pharaoh hastily sent for the two brothers, and cried out, "I have sinned this time: the Lord is righteous, and I and my people are wicked. Entreat the Lord (for it is enough) that there be no more mighty thunderings and hail; and I will let you go, and ye shall stay no longer." The answer was, "As soon as I am gone out of the city, I will spread abroad my hands unto the Lord; and the thunder shall cease, neither shall there be any more hail; that thou mayest know how that the earth is the Lord's. But as for thee and thy servants, I know that ye will not yet fear the Lord God."

Moses knew that the contest was not ended. Pharaoh's confessions and promises were not the effect of any radical change in his mind or heart, but were wrung from him by terror and anguish. Moses promised, however, to grant his request; for he would give him no occasion for further stubbornness. The prophet went forth, unheeding the fury of the tempest, and Pharaoh and all his host were witnesses to the power of Jehovah to preserve His messenger. Having passed without the city, Moses "spread abroad his hands unto the Lord: and the thunders and hail ceased, and the rain was not poured upon the earth." But no sooner had the king recovered from his fears than his heart returned to its perversity.

Then the Lord said unto Moses, "Go in unto Pharaoh: for I have hardened his heart, and the heart of his servants, that I might show these My signs before him; and that thou mayest tell in the ears of thy son, and of thy son's son, what things

The Egyptians were fast losing all that had been gained by the labor of the Hebrews.

I have wrought in Egypt, and My signs which I have done among them; that ye may know how that I am Jehovah." The Lord was manifesting His power, to confirm the faith of Israel in Him as the only true and living God. He would give unmistakable evidence of the difference He placed between them and the Egyptians, and would cause all nations to know that the Hebrews, whom they had despised and oppressed, were under the protection of the God of heaven.

Moses warned the monarch that if he still remained obstinate, a plague of locusts would be sent, which would cover the face of the earth and eat up every green thing that remained; they would fill the houses, even the palace itself; such a scourge, he said, as "neither thy fathers, nor thy fathers' fathers have seen, since the day that they were upon the earth unto this day."

The counselors of Pharaoh stood aghast. The nation had sustained great loss in the death of their cattle. Many of the people had been killed by the hail. The forests were broken down and the crops destroyed. They were fast losing all that had been gained by the labor of the Hebrews. The whole land was threatened with starvation. Princes and courtiers pressed about the king and angrily demanded, "How long shall this man be a snare unto us? let the men go, that they may serve the Lord their God: knowest thou not yet that Egypt is destroyed?"

Moses and Aaron were again summoned, and the monarch said to them, "Go, serve the Lord your God: but who are they that shall go?"

The answer was, "We will go with our young and with our old, with our sons and with our daughters, with our flocks and with our herds will we go; for we must hold a feast unto the Lord."

The king was filled with rage. "Let the Lord be so with you," he cried, "as I will let you go, and your little ones: look to it; for evil is before you. Not so: go now ye that are men, and serve the Lord; for that ye did desire. And they were driven out from Pharaoh's presence." Pharaoh had endeavored to destroy the Israelites by hard labor, but he now pretended to have a deep interest in their welfare and a tender care for their little ones. His real object was to keep the women and children as surety for the return of the men.

Moses now stretched forth his rod over the land, and an east wind blew, and brought locusts. "Very grievous were they; before them there were no such locusts as they, neither after them shall be such." They filled the sky till the land was darkened, and devoured every green thing remaining. Pharaoh sent for the prophets in haste, and said, "I have sinned against the Lord your God, and against you. Now therefore forgive, I pray thee, my sin only this once, and entreat the Lord your God, that He may take away from me this death only." They did so, and a strong west wind carried away the locusts toward the Red Sea. Still the king persisted in his stubborn resolution.

What Will Come Next? They Asked

The people of Egypt were ready to despair. The scourges that had already fallen upon them seemed almost beyond endurance, and they were filled with fear for the future. The nation had worshiped Pharaoh as a representative of their god, but many were now convinced that he was opposing himself to One who made all the powers of nature the ministers of His will. The Hebrew slaves, so miraculously favored, were becoming confident of deliverance. Their taskmasters dared not oppress them as heretofore. Throughout Egypt there was a secret fear that the enslaved race would rise and avenge their wrongs. Everywhere men were asking with bated breath, What will come next?

Suddenly a darkness settled upon the land, so thick and black that it seemed a "darkness which may be felt." Not only were the people deprived of light, but the atmosphere was very oppressive, so that breathing was difficult. "They saw not one another, neither rose any from his place for three days: but all the children of Israel had light in their dwellings." The sun and moon were objects of worship to the Egyptians; in this mysterious darkness the people and their gods alike were smitten by the power that had undertaken the cause of the bondmen. Yet fearful as it was, this judgment is an evidence of God's compassion and His unwillingness to destroy. He would give the people time for reflection and repentance before bringing upon them the last and most terrible of the plagues.

Fear at last wrung from Pharaoh a further concession. At the end of the third day of darkness he summoned Moses, and consented to the departure of the people, provided the flocks and herds were permitted to remain. "There shall not an hoof be left behind," replied the resolute Hebrew. "We know not with what we must serve the Lord, until we come thither." The king's anger burst forth beyond control. "Get thee from me," he cried, "take heed to thyself, see my face no more; for in that day thou seest my face thou shalt die."

The answer was, "Thou hast spoken well, I will see thy face again no more."

"The man Moses was very great in the land of Egypt, in the sight of Pharaoh's servants, and in the sight of the people." Moses was regarded with awe by the Egyptians. The king dared not harm him, for the people looked upon him as alone possessing power to remove the plagues. They desired that the Israelites might be permitted to leave Egypt. It was the king and the priests that opposed to the last the demands of Moses.

Publisher's Note:

Soon, we'll resume the magnificent story of Israel's deliverance. But first, we want to leap forward through the centuries from the past to the future—from the Old Testament book of Exodus to the New Testament book of Revelation. There, we'll notice the striking parallels between the plagues that fell on Egypt...and the very similar plagues yet to fall on the persecutors of God's people just before the return of Jesus to this earth.

Chapter 3

This chapter is based on Amos 8 and Revelation 16.

Flash Forward:
The Plagues Fall Yet Again

As the decree issued by the various rulers of Christendom against commandment keepers shall withdraw the protection of government and abandon them to those who desire their destruction, the people of God will flee from the cities and villages and associate together in companies, dwelling in the most desolate and solitary places. Many will find refuge in the strongholds of the mountains. Like the Christians of the Piedmont valleys, they will make the high places of the earth their sanctuaries and will thank God for "the munitions of rocks." Isaiah 33:16. But many of all nations and of all classes, high and low, rich and poor, black and white, will be cast into the most unjust and cruel bondage. The beloved of God pass weary days, bound in chains, shut in by prison bars, sentenced to be slain, some apparently left to die of starvation in dark and loathsome dungeons. No human ear is open to hear their moans; no human hand is ready to lend them help.

Will the Lord forget His people in this trying hour? Did He forget faithful Noah when judgments were visited upon the antediluvian world? Did He forget Lot when the fire came down from heaven to consume the cities of the plain? Did He forget Joseph surrounded by idolaters in Egypt? Did He forget Elijah when the oath of Jezebel threatened him with the fate of the prophets of Baal? Did He forget Jeremiah in the dark and dismal pit of his prison house? Did He forget the three worthies in the fiery furnace? or Daniel in the den of lions?

"Zion said, The Lord hath forsaken me, and my Lord hath forgotten me. Can a woman forget her sucking child, that she should not have compassion on the son of her womb? yea, they may forget, yet will I not forget thee. Behold, I have graven thee upon the palms of My hands." Isaiah 49:14-16. The Lord of hosts has said: "He that toucheth you toucheth the apple of His eye." Zechariah 2:8.

Though enemies may thrust them into prison, yet dungeon walls cannot cut off the communication between their souls and Christ. One who sees their every weakness, who is acquainted with every trial, is above all earthly powers; and angels will come to them in lonely cells, bringing light and peace from heaven. The prison will be as a palace; for the rich in faith dwell there, and the gloomy walls will be lighted up with heavenly light as when Paul and Silas prayed and sang praises at midnight in the Philippian dungeon.

God's judgments will be visited upon those who are seeking to oppress and destroy His people. His long forbearance with the wicked emboldens men in transgression, but their punishment is nonetheless certain and terrible because it is long delayed. "The Lord shall rise up as in Mount Perazim, He shall be wroth as in the valley of Gibeon, that He may do His work, His strange work; and bring to pass His act, His strange act." Isaiah 28:21. To our merciful God the act of punishment is a strange act. "As I live, saith the Lord God, I have no pleasure in the death of the wicked." Ezekiel 33:11. The Lord is "merciful and gracious, long-suffering, and abundant in goodness and truth, … forgiving iniquity and transgression and sin." Yet He will "by no means clear the guilty." The Lord is slow to anger, and great in power, and will not at all acquit the wicked." Exodus 34:6, 7; Nahum 1:3. By terrible things in righteousness He will vindicate the authority of His downtrodden law. The severity of the retribution awaiting the transgressor may be judged by the Lord's reluctance to execute justice. The nation with which He bears long, and which He will not smite until it has filled up the measure of its iniquity in God's account, will finally drink the cup of wrath unmixed with mercy.

Plagues More Terrible Than Those on Egypt

When Christ ceases His intercession in the sanctuary, the unmingled wrath threatened against those who worship the beast and his image and receive his mark (Revelation 14:9, 10), will be poured out. *The plagues upon Egypt when God was about to deliver Israel were similar in character to those more terrible and extensive judgments which are to fall upon the world just before the final deliverance of God's people.* [Emphasis supplied.] Says the revelator, in describing those terrific scourges: "There fell a noisome and grievous sore upon

In the final judgment, wrath is poured out unmixed with mercy.

the men which had the mark of the beast, and upon them which worshiped his image." The sea "became as the blood of a dead man: and every living soul died in the sea." And "the rivers and fountains of waters ... became blood." Terrible as these inflictions are, God's justice stands fully vindicated. The angel of God declares: "Thou art righteous, O Lord, ... because Thou hast judged thus. For they have shed the blood of saints and prophets, and Thou hast given them blood to drink; for they are worthy." Revelation 16:2-6. By condemning the people of God to death, they have as truly incurred the guilt of their blood as if it had been shed by their hands. In like manner Christ declared the Jews of His time guilty of all the blood of holy men which had been shed since the days of Abel; for they possessed the same spirit and were seeking to do the same work with these murderers of the prophets.

In the plague that follows, power is given to the sun "to scorch men with fire. And men were scorched with great heat." Verses 8, 9. The prophets thus describe the condition of the earth at this fearful time: "The land mourneth; ... because the harvest of the field is perished. ... All the trees of the field are withered: because joy is withered away from the sons of men." "The seed is rotten under their clods, the garners are laid desolate. ... How do the beasts groan! the herds of cattle are perplexed, because they have no pasture. ... The rivers of water are dried up, and the fire hath devoured the pastures of the wilderness." "The songs of the temple shall be howlings in that day, saith the Lord God: there shall be many dead bodies in every place; they shall cast them forth with silence." Joel 1:10-12, 17-20; Amos 8:3.

These plagues are not universal, or the inhabitants of the earth would be wholly cut off. Yet they will be the most awful scourges that have ever been known to mortals. All the judgments upon men, prior to the close of probation, have been mingled with mercy. The pleading blood of Christ has shielded the sinner from receiving the full measure of his guilt; but in the final judgment, wrath is poured out unmixed with mercy.

In that day, multitudes will desire the shelter of God's mercy which they have so long despised. "Behold, the days come, saith the

Lord God, that I will send a famine in the land, not a famine of bread, nor a thirst for water, but of hearing the words of the Lord: and they shall wander from sea to sea, and from the north even to the east, they shall run to and fro to seek the word of the Lord, and shall not find it." Amos 8:11, 12.

The people of God will not be free from suffering; but while persecuted and distressed, while they endure privation and suffer for want of food they will not be left to perish. That God who cared for Elijah will not pass by one of His self-sacrificing children. He who numbers the hairs of their head will care for them, and in time of famine they shall be satisfied. While the wicked are dying from hunger and pestilence, angels will shield the righteous and supply their wants. To him that "walketh righteously" is the promise: "Bread shall be given him; his waters shall be sure." "When the poor and needy seek water, and there is none, and their tongue faileth for thirst, I the Lord will hear them, I the God of Israel will not forsake them." Isaiah 33:15, 16; 41:17.

> *God who cared for Elijah will not pass by one of His self-sacrificing children.*
>

"Although the fig tree shall not blossom, neither shall fruit be in the vines; the labor of the olive shall fail, and the fields shall yield no meat; the flock shall be cut off from the fold, and there shall be no herd in the stalls;" yet shall they that fear Him "rejoice in the Lord" and joy in the God of their salvation. Habakkuk 3:17, 18.

"The Lord is thy keeper: the Lord is thy shade upon thy right hand. The sun shall not smite thee by day, nor the moon by night. The Lord shall preserve thee from all evil: He shall preserve thy soul." "He shall deliver thee from the snare of the fowler, and from the noisome pestilence. He shall cover thee with His feathers, and under His wings shalt thou trust: His truth shall be thy shield and buckler. Thou shalt not be afraid for the terror by night; nor for the arrow that flieth by day; nor for the pestilence that walketh in darkness; nor for the destruction that wasteth at noonday. A thousand shall fall at thy side, and ten thousand at thy right hand; but it shall not come nigh thee. Only with thine eyes shalt thou behold and see the reward of the wicked. Because thou hast made the Lord, which is my refuge, even the Most High, thy habitation; there shall no evil befall thee, neither shall any plague come nigh thy dwelling." Psalms 121:5-7; 91:3-10.

Yet to human sight it will appear that the people of God must soon seal their testimony with their blood as did the martyrs before them. They themselves begin to fear that the Lord has left them to fall by the hand of their enemies. It is a time of fearful agony. Day and night they cry unto God for deliverance. The wicked exult, and the jeering cry is heard: "Where now is your faith? Why does not God deliver you out of our hands if you are indeed His people?" But the waiting ones remember Jesus dying upon Calvary's cross and the chief priests and rulers shouting in mockery: "He saved others; Himself He cannot save. If He be the King of Israel, let Him now come down from the cross, and we will believe Him." Matthew 27:42. Like Jacob, all are wrestling with God. Their countenances express their internal struggle. Paleness sits upon every face. Yet they cease not their earnest intercession.

Could men see with heavenly vision, they would behold companies of angels that excel in strength stationed about those who have kept the word of Christ's patience. With sympathizing tenderness, angels have witnessed their distress and have heard their prayers. They are waiting the word of their Commander to snatch them from their peril. But they must wait yet a little longer. The people of God must drink of the cup and be baptized with the baptism. The very delay, so painful to them, is the best answer to their petitions. As they endeavor to wait trustingly for the Lord to work they are led to exercise faith, hope, and patience, which have been too little exercised during their religious experience. Yet for the elect's sake the time of trouble will be shortened. "Shall not God avenge His own elect, which cry day and night unto Him? ... I tell you that He will avenge them speedily." Luke 18:7, 8. The end will come more quickly than men expect. The wheat will be gathered and bound in sheaves for the garner of God; the tares will be bound as fagots for the fires of destruction.

> *For the elect's sake, the time of trouble will be shortened.*
>
>

The heavenly sentinels, faithful to their trust, continue their watch. Though a general decree has fixed the time when commandment keepers may be put to death, their enemies will in some cases anticipate the decree, and before the time specified, will endeavor to take their lives. But none can pass the mighty guardians stationed about every faithful soul. Some are assailed in their flight from the cities and villages; but the swords raised against them break and fall powerless as a straw. Others are defended by angels in the form of men of war.

The Ministry of Angels

In all ages, God has wrought through holy angels for the succor and deliverance of His people. Celestial beings have taken an active part in the affairs of men. They have appeared clothed in garments that shone as the lightning; they have come as men in the garb of wayfarers. Angels have appeared in human form to men of God. They have rested, as if weary, under the oaks at noon. They have accepted the hospitalities of human homes. They have acted as guides to benighted travelers. They have, with their own hands, kindled the fires at the altar. They have opened prison doors and set free the servants of the Lord. Clothed with the panoply of heaven, they came to roll away the stone from the Saviour's tomb.

In the form of men, angels are often in the assemblies of the righteous; and they visit the assemblies of the wicked, as they went to Sodom, to make a record of their deeds, to determine whether they have passed the boundary of God's forbearance. The Lord delights in mercy; and for the sake of a few who really serve Him, He restrains calamities and prolongs the tranquillity of multitudes. Little do sinners against God realize that they are indebted for their own lives to the faithful few whom they delight to ridicule and oppress.

Though the rulers of this world know it not, yet often in their councils angels have been spokesmen. Human eyes have looked upon them; human ears have listened to their appeals; human lips have opposed their suggestions and ridiculed their counsels; human hands have met them with insult and abuse. In the council hall and the court of justice these heavenly messengers have shown an intimate acquaintance with human history; they have proved themselves better able to plead the cause of the oppressed than were their ablest and most eloquent defenders. They have defeated purposes and arrested evils that would have greatly retarded the work of God and would have caused great suffering to His people. In the hour of peril and distress "the angel of the Lord encampeth round about them that fear Him, and delivereth them." Psalm 34:7.

With earnest longing, God's people await the tokens of their coming King. As the watchmen are accosted, "What of the night?" the answer is given unfalteringly, "The morning cometh, and also the night." Isaiah 21:11, 12. Light is gleaming upon the clouds above the mountaintops. Soon there will be a revealing of His glory. The Sun of Righteousness is about to shine forth. The morning and the night are both at hand—the opening of endless day to the righteous, the settling down of eternal night to the wicked."

The Lord permits conflicts, to prepare the soul for peace.

As the wrestling ones urge their petitions before God, the veil separating them from the unseen seems almost withdrawn. The heavens glow with the dawning of eternal day, and like the melody of angel songs the words fall upon the ear: "Stand fast to your allegiance. Help is coming." Christ, the almighty Victor, holds out to His weary soldiers a crown of immortal glory; and His voice comes from the gates ajar: "Lo, I am with you. Be not afraid. I am acquainted with all your sorrows; I have borne your griefs. You are not warring against untried enemies. I have fought the battle in your behalf, and in My name you are more than conquerors."

The precious Saviour will send help just when we need it. The way to heaven is consecrated by His footprints. Every thorn that wounds our feet has wounded His. Every cross that we are called to bear He has borne before us. The Lord permits conflicts, to prepare the soul for peace. The time of trouble is a fearful ordeal for God's people; but it is the time for every true believer to look up, and by faith he may see the bow of promise encircling him.

The redeemed of the Lord shall return, and come with singing unto Zion; and everlasting joy shall be upon their head: they shall obtain gladness and joy; and sorrow and mourning shall flee away. I, even I, am He that comforteth you: who art thou, that thou shouldest be afraid of a man that shall die, and of the son of man which shall be made as grass; and forgettest the Lord thy Maker; … and hast feared continually every day because of the fury of the oppressor, as if he were ready to destroy? and where is the fury of the oppressor? The captive exile hasteneth that he may be loosed, and that he should not die in the pit, nor that his bread should fail. But I am the Lord thy God, that divided the sea, whose waves roared: The Lord of hosts is His name. And I have put My words in thy mouth, and I have covered thee in the shadow of Mine hand. Isaiah 51:11-16.

Therefore hear now this, thou afflicted, and drunken, but not with wine: Thus saith thy Lord the Lord, and thy God that pleadeth the cause of His people, Behold, I have taken out of thine hand the cup of trembling, even the dregs of the cup of My fury; thou shalt no more drink it again: but I will put it into the hand of them that afflict thee; which have said to thy soul, Bow down, that we may go over: and thou hast laid thy body as the ground, and as the street, to them that went over. Verses 21-23.

The eye of God, looking down the ages, was fixed upon the crisis which His people are to meet, when earthly powers shall be arrayed against them. Like the captive exile, they will be in fear of death by starvation or by violence. But the Holy One who divided the Red Sea before Israel, will manifest His mighty power and turn their captivity. "They shall be Mine, saith the Lord of hosts, in that day when I make up My jewels; and I will spare them, as a man spareth his own son that serveth him." Malachi 3:17. If the blood of Christ's faithful witnesses were shed at this time, it would not, like the blood of the martyrs, be as seed sown to yield a harvest for God. Their fidelity would not be a testimony to convince others of the truth; for the obdurate heart has beaten back the waves of mercy until they return no more. If the righteous were now left to fall a prey to their enemies, it would be a triumph for the prince of darkness. Says the psalmist: "In the time of trouble He shall hide me in His pavilion: in the secret of His tabernacle shall He hide me." Psalm 27:5. Christ has spoken: "Come, My people, enter thou into thy chambers, and shut thy doors about thee: hide thyself as it were for a little moment, until the indignation be overpast. For, behold, the Lord cometh out of His place to punish the inhabitants of the earth for their iniquity." Isaiah 26:20, 21. Glorious will be the deliverance of those who have patiently waited for His coming and whose names are written in the book of life.

Part 2

The Great Deliverance

God Made the Sea Into Dry Land

Then Moses stretched out his hand over the sea; and the Lord caused the sea to go back by a strong east wind all that night, and made the sea into dry land, and the waters were divided. So the children of Israel went into the midst of the sea on the dry ground, and the waters were a wall to them on their right hand and on their left. And the Egyptians pursued and went after them into the midst of the sea, all Pharaoh's horses, his chariots, and his horsemen.

Then the Lord said to Moses, "Stretch out your hand over the sea, that the waters may come back upon the Egyptians, on their chariots, and on their horsemen." And Moses stretched out his hand over the sea; and when the morning appeared, the sea returned to its full depth, while the Egyptians were fleeing into it. So the Lord overthrew the Egyptians in the midst of the sea. Then the waters returned and covered the chariots, the horsemen, and all the army of Pharaoh that came into the sea after them. Not so much as one of them remained.

—Exodus 14:21–23, 26–28

Part 2

Thought Questions

- On Passover evening, Israelites were to place the blood of a flawless animal on their doorposts. God said that when He saw the blood, He would "pass over you, and the plague shall not be upon you to destroy you." Does this symbolize to you that when God sees the blood of Jesus covering you, the plague of death will not destroy you?

- Sometimes in life, we—like the Israelites—come to a place where we are surrounded on all sides with nowhere left to go. Yet God says to us what He said to them: "Go forward!" Have you ever heard God say this to you? And what was the outcome?

- The Great Deliverance of Israel was a preview of the Great Deliverance of God's people at the very end of time. Think now about this seriously: What can we each do, each day, to be sure we're among those delivered when that day comes — and not among those God passes by?

Chapter 4

This chapter is based on Exodus 11; 12:1–32.

Final Night in Egypt: Passover

When the demand for Israel's release had been first presented to the king of Egypt, the warning of the most terrible of the plagues had been given. Moses was directed
to say to Pharaoh, "Thus saith the Lord, Israel is My son, even My
first-born: and I say unto thee, Let My son go, that he may serve Me:
and if thou refuse to let him go, behold, I will slay thy son, even thy
first-born." Exodus 4:22, 23. Though despised by the Egyptians, the
Israelites had been honored by God, in that they were singled out to
be the depositaries of His law. In the special blessings and privileges accorded them, they had pre-eminence among the nations, as the
first-born son had among brothers.

The judgment of which Egypt had first been warned, was to be
the last visited. God is long-suffering and plenteous in mercy. He has
a tender care for the beings formed in His image. If the loss of their
harvests and their flocks and herds had brought Egypt to repentance,
the children would not have been smitten; but the nation had stubbornly resisted the divine command, and now the final blow was
about to fall.

Moses had been forbidden, on pain of death, to appear again in
Pharaoh's presence; but a last message from God was to be delivered
to the rebellious monarch, and again Moses came before him, with
the terrible announcement: "Thus saith the Lord, About midnight
will I go out into the midst of Egypt: and all the first-born in the land
of Egypt shall die, from the first-born of Pharaoh that sitteth upon
his throne, even unto the first-born of the maidservant that is behind
the mill; and all the first-born of beasts. And there shall be a great cry
throughout all the land of Egypt, such as there was none like it, nor
shall be like it any more. But against any of the children of Israel shall
not a dog move his tongue, against man or beast: that ye may know
how that the Lord doth put a difference between the Egyptians and

Israel. And all these thy servants shall come down unto me, and bow down themselves unto me, saying, Get thee out, and all the people that follow thee: and after that I will go out."

When I See the Blood, I Will Pass Over You

Before the execution of this sentence the Lord through Moses gave direction to the children of Israel concerning their departure from Egypt, and especially for their preservation from the coming judgment. Each family, alone or in connection with others, was to slay a lamb or a kid "without blemish," and with a bunch of hyssop sprinkle its blood on "the two side posts and on the upper doorpost" of the house, that the destroying angel, coming at midnight, might not enter that dwelling. They were to eat the flesh roasted, with unleavened bread and bitter herbs, at night, as Moses said, "with your loins girded, your shoes on your feet, and your staff in your hand; and ye shall eat it in haste: it is the Lord's Passover."

The Lord declared: "I will pass through the land of Egypt this night, and will smite all the first-born in the land of Egypt, both man and beast; and against all the gods of Egypt I will execute judgment. ... And the blood shall be to you for a token upon the houses where ye are: and when I see the blood, I will pass over you, and the plague shall not be upon you to destroy you, when I smite the land of Egypt."

In commemoration of this great deliverance a feast was to be observed yearly by the people of Israel in all future generations. "This day shall be unto you for a memorial; and ye shall keep it a feast to the Lord throughout your generations: ye shall keep it a feast by an ordinance forever." As they should keep the feast in future years, they were to repeat to their children the story of this great deliverance, as Moses bade them: "Ye shall say, It is the sacrifice of the Lord's Passover, who passed over the houses of the children of Israel in Egypt, when He smote the Egyptians, and delivered our houses."

Furthermore, the first-born of both man and beast were to be the Lord's, to be bought back only by a ransom, in acknowledgment that when the first-born in Egypt perished, that of Israel, though graciously preserved, had been justly exposed to the same doom but for the atoning sacrifice. "All the first-born are Mine," the Lord declared;

"for on the day that I smote all the first-born in the land of Egypt, I hallowed unto Me all the first-born in Israel, both man and beast: Mine they shall be," Numbers 3:13. After the institution of the tabernacle service the Lord chose unto Himself the tribe of Levi for the work of the sanctuary, instead of the first-born of the people. "They are wholly given unto Me from among the children of Israel," He said. "Instead of the first-born of all the children of Israel, have I taken them unto Me." Numbers 8:16. All the people were, however, still required, in acknowledgment of God's mercy, to pay a redemption price for the first-born son. Numbers 18:15, 16.

The Passover was to be both commemorative and typical, not only pointing back to the deliverance from Egypt, but forward to the greater deliverance which Christ was to accomplish in freeing His people from the bondage of sin. The sacrificial lamb represents "the Lamb of God," in whom is our only hope of salvation. Says the apostle, "Christ our Passover is sacrificed for us." 1 Corinthians 5:7. It was not enough that the paschal lamb be slain; its blood must be sprinkled upon the doorposts; so the merits of Christ's blood must be applied to the soul. We must believe, not only that He died for the world, but that He died for us individually. We must appropriate to ourselves the virtue of the atoning sacrifice.

> *We must believe, not only that He died for the world, but that He died for us individually.*
>
>

The hyssop used in sprinkling the blood was the symbol of purification, being thus employed in the cleansing of the leper and of those defiled by contact with the dead. In the psalmist's prayer also its significance is seen: "Purge me with hyssop, and I shall be clean: wash me, and I shall be whiter than snow." Psalm 51:7.

The lamb was to be prepared whole, not a bone of it being broken: so not a bone was to be broken of the Lamb of God, who was to die for us. John 19:36. Thus was also represented the completeness of Christ's sacrifice.

The flesh was to be eaten. It is not enough even that we believe on Christ for the forgiveness of sin; we must by faith be constantly receiving spiritual strength and nourishment from Him through His word. Said Christ, "Except ye eat the flesh of the Son of man, and drink His blood, ye have no life in you. Whoso eateth My flesh, and drinketh My blood, hath eternal life." John 6:53, 54. And to explain His meaning He said, "The words that I speak unto you, they are spirit, and they are life." Verse 63. Jesus accepted His Father's law, wrought out its principles in His life, manifested its spirit, and showed its beneficent power in the heart. Says John, "The Word was made flesh, and dwelt among us, (and we beheld His glory, the glory as of the only begotten of the Father,) full of grace and truth." John 1:14. The followers of Christ must be partakers of His experience. They must receive and assimilate the word of God so that it shall become the motive power of life and action. By the power of Christ they must be changed into His likeness, and reflect the divine attributes. They must eat the flesh and drink the blood of the Son of God, or there is no life in them. The spirit and work of Christ must become the spirit and work of His disciples.

The lamb was to be eaten with bitter herbs, as pointing back to the bitterness of the bondage in Egypt. So when we feed upon Christ, it should be with contrition of heart, because of our sins. The use of unleavened bread also was significant. It was expressly enjoined in the law of the Passover, and as strictly observed by the Jews in their practice, that no leaven should be found in their houses during the feast. In like manner the leaven of sin must be put away from all who would receive life and nourishment from Christ. So Paul writes to the Corinthian church, "Purge out therefore the old leaven, that ye may be a new lump. ... For even Christ our Passover is sacrificed for us: therefore let us keep the feast, not with old leaven, neither with the leaven of malice and wickedness; but with the unleavened bread of sincerity and truth." 1 Corinthians 5:7, 8.

> *When we feed upon Christ, it should be with contrition of heart, because of our sins.*

Before obtaining freedom, the bondmen must show their faith in the great deliverance about to be accomplished. The token of blood must be placed upon their houses, and they must separate themselves and their families from the Egyptians, and gather within their own dwellings. Had the Israelites disregarded in any particular the directions given them, had they neglected to separate their children from the Egyptians, had they slain the lamb, but failed to strike the door-post with blood, or had any gone out of their houses, they would not have been secure. They might have honestly believed that they had done all that was necessary, but their sincerity would not have saved them. All who failed to heed the Lord's directions would lose their first-born by the hand of the destroyer.

By obedience the people were to give evidence of their faith. So all who hope to be saved by the merits of the blood of Christ should realize that they themselves have something to do in securing their salvation. While it is Christ only that can redeem us from the penalty of transgression, we are to turn from sin to obedience. Man is to be saved by faith, not by works; yet his faith must be shown by his works. God has given His Son to die as a propitiation for sin, He has manifested the light of truth, the way of life, He has given facilities, ordinances, and privileges; and now man must co-operate with these saving agencies; he must appreciate and use the helps that God has provided—believe and obey all the divine requirements.

As Moses rehearsed to Israel the provisions of God for their deliverance, "the people bowed the head and worshiped." The glad hope of freedom, the awful knowledge of the impending judgment upon their oppressors, the cares and labors incident to their speedy departure—all were for the time swallowed up in gratitude to their gracious Deliverer. Many of the Egyptians had been led to acknowledge the God of the Hebrews as the only true God, and these now begged to be permitted to find shelter in the homes of Israel when the destroying angel should pass through the land. They were gladly welcomed, and they pledged themselves henceforth to serve the God of Jacob and to go forth from Egypt with His people.

Departure Preparations; a Midnight Cry

The Israelites obeyed the directions that God had given. Swiftly and secretly they made their preparations for departure. Their families were gathered, the paschal lamb slain, the flesh roasted with fire, the unleavened bread and bitter herbs prepared. The father and priest of the household sprinkled the blood upon the doorpost, and joined his family within the dwelling. In haste and silence the paschal lamb was eaten. In awe the people prayed and watched, the heart of the eldest born, from the strong man down to the little child, throbbing with indefinable dread. Fathers and mothers clasped in their arms their loved first-born as they thought of the fearful stroke that was to fall that night. But no dwelling of Israel was visited by the death-dealing angel. The sign of blood—the sign of a Saviour's protection—was on their doors, and the destroyer entered not.

At midnight "there was a great cry in Egypt: for there was not a house where there was not one dead." All the first-born in the land, "from the firstborn of Pharaoh that sat on his throne unto the first-born of the captive that was in the dungeon; and all the firstborn of cattle" had been smitten by the destroyer. Throughout the vast realm of Egypt the pride of every household had been laid low. The shrieks and wails of the mourners filled the air. King and courtiers, with blanched faces and trembling limbs, stood aghast at the overmastering horror. Pharaoh remembered how he had once exclaimed, "Who is Jehovah, that I should obey His voice to let Israel go? I know not Jehovah, neither will I let Israel go." Now, his heaven-daring pride humbled in the dust, he "called for Moses and Aaron by night, and said, Rise up, and get you forth from among my people, both ye and the children of Israel; and go, serve the Lord, as ye have said. Also take your flocks and your herds, as ye have said. ... And be gone; and bless me also." The royal counselors also and the people entreated the Israelites to depart "out of the land in haste; for they said, We be all dead men."

Chapter 5

This chapter is based on Exodus 12:34–51; 13–15.

Through the Sea to Freedom

With their loins girt, with sandaled feet, and staff in hand, the people of Israel had stood, hushed, awed, yet expectant, awaiting the royal mandate that should bid them go forth. Before the morning broke, they were on their way. During the plagues, as the manifestation of God's power had kindled faith in the hearts of the bondmen and had struck terror to their oppressors, the Israelites had gradually assembled themselves in Goshen; and notwithstanding the suddenness of their flight, some provision had already been made for the necessary organization and control of the moving multitudes, they being divided into companies, under appointed leaders.

And they went out, "about six hundred thousand on foot that were men, beside children. And a mixed multitude went up also with them." In this multitude were not only those who were actuated by faith in the God of Israel, but also a far greater number who desired only to escape from the plagues, or who followed in the wake of the moving multitudes merely from excitement and curiosity. This class were ever a hindrance and a snare to Israel.

The people took also with them "flocks, and herds, even very much cattle." These were the property of the Israelites, who had never sold their possessions to the king, as had the Egyptians. Jacob and his sons had brought their flocks and herds with them to Egypt, where they had greatly increased. Before leaving Egypt, the people, by the direction of Moses, claimed a recompense for their unpaid labor; and the Egyptians were too eager to be freed from their presence to refuse them. The bondmen went forth laden with the spoil of their oppressors.

That day completed the history revealed to Abraham in prophetic vision centuries before: "Thy seed shall be a stranger in a land that is not theirs, and shall serve them; and they shall afflict them four hundred years; and also that nation, whom they shall serve, will I judge: and afterward shall they come out with great substance." Genesis 15:13, 14. The four hundred years had been fulfilled. "And it came to pass the self-same day, that the Lord did bring the children of Israel out of the land of Egypt by their armies." In their departure from Egypt the Israelites bore with them a precious legacy, in the bones of Joseph, which had so long awaited the fulfillment of God's promise, and which, during the dark years of bondage, had been a reminder of Israel's deliverance.

Instead of pursuing the direct route to Canaan, which lay through the country of the Philistines, the Lord directed their course southward, toward the shores of the Red Sea. "For God said, Lest peradventure the people repent when they see war, and they return to Egypt." Had they attempted to pass through Philistia, their progress would have been opposed; for the Philistines, regarding them as slaves escaping from their masters, would not have hesitated to make war upon them. The Israelites were poorly prepared for an encounter with that powerful and warlike people. They had little knowledge of God and little faith in Him, and they would have become terrified and disheartened. They were unarmed and unaccustomed to war, their spirits were depressed by long bondage, and they were encumbered with women and children, flocks and herds. In leading them by the way of the Red Sea, the Lord revealed Himself as a God of compassion as well as of judgment.

"And they took their journey from Succoth, and encamped in Etham, in the edge of the wilderness. And the Lord went before them by day in a pillar of cloud, to lead them the way; and by night in a pillar of fire, to give them light; to go by day and night. He took not away the pillar of the cloud by day, nor the pillar of fire by night, from before the people." Says the psalmist, "He spread a cloud for a covering; and fire to give light in the night." Psalm 105:39. See also I Corinthians 10:1, 2. The standard of their invisible Leader was ever with them. By day the cloud directed their journeyings or spread as a canopy above the host. It served as a protection from the burning heat, and by its coolness and moisture afforded grateful refreshment in the parched, thirsty desert. By night it became a pillar of fire, illuminating their encampment and constantly assuring them of the divine presence.

In one of the most beautiful and comforting passages of Isaiah's prophecy, reference is made to the pillar of cloud and of fire to represent God's care for His people in the great final struggle with the powers of evil: "The Lord will create upon every dwelling place of Mount Zion, and upon her assemblies, a cloud and smoke by day, and the shining of a flaming fire by night: for above all the glory shall be a covering. And there shall be a tabernacle for a shadow in the daytime from the heat, and for a place of refuge, and for a covert from storm and from rain." Isaiah 4:5, 6, margin.

Across a dreary, desertlike expanse they journeyed. Already they began to wonder whither their course would lead; they were becoming weary with the toilsome way, and in some hearts began to arise a fear of pursuit by the Egyptians. But the cloud went forward, and they followed. And now the Lord directed Moses to turn aside into a rocky defile, and encamp beside the sea. It was revealed to him that Pharaoh would pursue them, but that God would be honored in their deliverance.

In Egypt the report was spread that the children of Israel, instead of tarrying to worship in the desert, were pressing on toward the Red Sea. Pharaoh's counselors declared to the king that their bondmen had fled, never to return. The people deplored their folly in attributing the death of the first-born to the power of God. Their great men, recovering from their fears, accounted for the plagues as the result of natural causes. "Why have we done this, that we have let Israel go from serving us?" was the bitter cry.

Israel Hemmed in on All Sides

Pharaoh collected his forces, "six hundred chosen chariots, and all the chariots of Egypt," horsemen, captains, and foot soldiers. The king himself, attended by the great men of his realm, headed the attacking army. To secure the favor of the gods, and thus ensure the success of their undertaking, the priests also accompanied them. The king was resolved to intimidate the Israelites by a grand display of his power. The Egyptians feared lest their forced submission to the God of Israel should subject them to the derision of other nations; but if they should now go forth with a great show of power and bring back the fugitives, they would redeem their glory, as well as recover the services of their bondmen.

The Hebrews were encamped beside the sea, whose waters presented a seemingly impassable barrier before them, while on the south a rugged mountain obstructed their further progress. Suddenly they beheld in the distance the flashing armor and moving chariots betokening the advance guard of a great army. As the force drew nearer, the hosts of Egypt were seen in full pursuit. Terror filled the hearts of Israel. Some cried unto the Lord, but far the greater part hastened to Moses with their complaints: "Because there were no graves in Egypt, hast thou taken us away to die in the wilderness? wherefore hast thou dealt thus with us, to carry us forth out of Egypt? Is not this the word that we did tell thee in Egypt, saying, Let us alone, that we may serve the Egyptians? For it had been better for us to serve the Egyptians, than that we should die in the wilderness."

To Israel, Moses said: "Fear ye not, stand still, and see the salvation of the Lord."

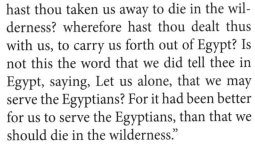

Moses was greatly troubled that his people should manifest so little faith in God, notwithstanding they had repeatedly witnessed the manifestation of His power in their behalf. How could they charge upon him the dangers and difficulties of their situation, when he had followed the express command of God? True, there was no possibility of deliverance unless God Himself should interpose for their release; but having been brought into this position in obedience to the divine direction, Moses felt no fear of the consequences. His calm and assuring reply to the people was, "Fear ye not, stand still, and see the salvation of the Lord, which He will show to you today: for the Egyptians whom ye have seen today, ye shall see them again no more forever. The Lord shall fight for you, and ye shall hold your peace."

It was not an easy thing to hold the hosts of Israel in waiting before the Lord. Lacking discipline and self-control, they became violent and unreasonable. They expected speedily to fall into the hands of their oppressors, and their wailings and lamentations were loud and deep. The wonderful pillar of cloud had been followed as the signal of God to go forward; but now they questioned among themselves if it might not foreshadow some great calamity; for had it not led them on the wrong side of the mountain, into an impassable way? Thus the angel of God appeared to their deluded minds as the harbinger of disaster.

But now, as the Egyptian host approached them, expecting to make them an easy prey, the cloudy column rose majestically into the heavens, passed over the Israelites, and descended between them and the armies of Egypt. A wall of darkness interposed between the pursued and their pursuers. The Egyptians could no longer discern the camp of the Hebrews, and were forced to halt. But as the darkness of night deepened, the wall of cloud became a great light to the Hebrews, flooding the entire encampment with the radiance of day.

Then hope returned to the hearts of Israel. And Moses lifted up his voice unto the Lord. "And the Lord said unto Moses, Wherefore criest thou unto Me? speak unto the children of Israel, that they go forward. But lift thou up thy rod, and stretch out thine hand over the sea, and divide it: and the children of Israel shall go on dry ground through the midst of the sea."

The psalmist, describing the passage of the sea by Israel, sang, "Thy way was in the sea, and Thy paths in the great waters, and Thy footsteps were not known. Thou leddest Thy people like a flock, by the hand of Moses and Aaron." Psalm 77:19, 20, R.V. As Moses stretched out his rod the waters parted, and Israel went into the midst of the sea, upon dry ground, while the waters stood like a wall upon each side. The light from God's pillar of fire shone upon the foam-capped billows, and lighted the road that was cut like a mighty furrow through the waters of the sea, and was lost in the obscurity of the farther shore.

> *The waters parted, and Israel went into the midst of the sea, upon dry ground.*
>
>

"The Egyptians pursued, and went in after them to the midst of the sea, even all Pharaoh's horses, his chariots, and his horsemen. And it came to pass, that in the morning watch the Lord looked unto the host of the Egyptians through the pillar of fire and of the cloud, and troubled the host of the Egyptians." The mysterious cloud changed to a pillar of fire before their astonished eyes. The thunders pealed and the lightnings flashed. "The clouds poured out water; the skies sent out a sound: Thine arrows also went abroad. The voice of Thy thunder was in the whirlwind; the lightning lightened the world: the earth trembled and shook." Psalm 77:17, 18, R.V.

The Egyptians were seized with confusion and dismay. Amid the wrath of the elements, in which they heard the voice of an angry God, they endeavored to retrace their steps and flee to the shore they had quitted. But Moses stretched out his rod, and the piled-up waters, hissing, roaring, and eager for their prey, rushed together and swallowed the Egyptian army in their black depths.

As morning broke it revealed to the multitudes of Israel all that remained of their mighty foes—the mail-clad bodies cast upon the shore. From the most terrible peril, one night had brought complete deliverance. That vast, helpless throng—bondmen unused to battle, women, children, and cattle, with the sea before them, and the mighty armies of Egypt pressing behind—had seen their path opened through the waters and their enemies overwhelmed in the moment of expected triumph. Jehovah alone had brought them deliverance, and to Him their hearts were turned in gratitude and faith. Their emotion found utterance in songs of praise. The Spirit of God rested upon Moses, and he led the people in a triumphant anthem of thanksgiving, the earliest and one of the most sublime that are known to man.

The Song of Moses—a Song of Deliverence

I will sing unto Jehovah, for He hath triumphed gloriously;
The horse and his rider hath He thrown into the sea.
The Lord is my strength and my song,
And He is become my salvation:
This is my God, and I will praise Him;
My father's God, and I will exalt Him.
The Lord is a man of war:
Jehovah is His name.
Pharaoh's chariots and his host hath He cast into the sea:
And his chosen captains are sunk in the Red Sea.
The deeps cover them:
They went down into the depths like a stone.
Thy right hand, O Lord, is glorious in power,
Thy right hand, O Lord, dasheth in pieces the enemy. ...
Who is like unto Thee, O Lord, among the gods?

Who is like Thee, glorious in holiness,

Fearful in praises, doing wonders? ...

Thou in Thy mercy hast led the people which Thou has redeemed:

Thou hast guided them in Thy strength to Thy holy habitation.

The peoples have heard, they tremble. ...

Terror and dread falleth upon them;

By the greatness of Thine arm they are as still as a stone;

Till Thy people pass over, O Lord,

Till the people pass over which Thou hast purchased.

Thou shalt bring them in, and plant them in the mountain of Thine inheritance,

The place, O Lord, which Thou hast made for Thee to dwell in.

—Exodus 15:1–16, R.V.

Like the voice of the great deep, rose from the vast hosts of Israel that sublime ascription. It was taken up by the women of Israel, Miriam, the sister of Moses, leading the way, as they went forth with timbrel and dance. Far over desert and sea rang the joyous refrain, and the mountains re-echoed the words of their praise—"Sing ye to Jehovah, for He hath triumphed gloriously."

This song and the great deliverance which it commemorates, made an impression never to be effaced from the memory of the Hebrew people. From age to age it was echoed by the prophets and singers of Israel, testifying that Jehovah is the strength and deliverance of those who trust in Him. That song does not belong to the Jewish people alone. It points forward to the destruction of all the foes of righteousness and the final victory of the Israel of God. The prophet of Patmos beholds the white-robed multitude that have "gotten the victory," standing on the "sea of glass mingled with fire," having "the harps of God. And they sing the song of Moses the servant of God, and the song of the Lamb." Revelation 15:2, 3.

"Not unto us, O Lord, not unto us, but unto Thy name give glory, for Thy mercy, and for Thy truth's sake." Psalm 115:1. Such was the spirit that pervaded Israel's song of deliverance, and it is the spirit that should dwell in the hearts of all who love and fear God. In freeing out souls from the bondage of sin, God has wrought for us a deliverance greater than that of the Hebrews at the Red Sea. Like the Hebrew host, we should praise the Lord with heart and soul and voice for His "wonderful works to the children of men." Those who dwell upon God's great mercies, and are not unmindful of His lesser gifts, will put on the girdle of gladness and make melody in their hearts to the Lord. The daily blessings that we receive from the hand of God, and above all else the death of Jesus to bring happiness and heaven within our reach, should be a theme for constant gratitude. What compassion, what matchless love, has God shown to us, lost sinners, in connecting us with Himself, to be to Him a peculiar treasure! What a sacrifice has been made by our Redeemer, that we may be called children of God! We should praise God for the blessed hope held out before us in the great plan of redemption, we should praise Him for the heavenly inheritance and for His rich promises; praise Him that Jesus lives to intercede for us.

"Whoso offereth praise," says the Creator, "glorifieth Me." Psalm 50:23. All the inhabitants of heaven unite in praising God. Let us learn the song of the angels now, that we may sing it when we join their shining ranks. Let us say with the psalmist, "While I live will I praise the Lord: I will sing praises unto my God while I have any being." "Let the people praise Thee, O God; let all the people praise Thee." Psalms 146:2; 67:5.

God in His providence brought the Hebrews into the mountain fastnesses before the sea, that He might manifest His power in their deliverance and signally humble the pride of their oppressors. He might have saved them in any other way, but He chose this method in order to test their faith and strengthen their trust in Him. The people were weary and terrified, yet if they had held back when Moses bade them advance, God would never have opened the path for them. It was "by faith" that "they passed through the Red Sea as by dry land." Hebrews 11:29. In marching down to the very water, they showed that they believed the word of God as spoken by Moses. They did all that was in their power to do, and then the Mighty One of Israel divided the sea to make a path for their feet.

The great lesson here taught is for all time. Often the Christian life is beset by dangers, and duty seems hard to perform. The imagination pictures impending ruin before and bondage or death behind. Yet the voice of God speaks clearly, "Go forward." We should obey this command, even though our eyes cannot penetrate the darkness, and we feel the cold waves about our feet. The obstacles that hinder our progress will never disappear before a halting, doubting spirit. Those who defer obedience till every shadow of uncertainty disappears and there remains no risk of failure or defeat, will never obey at all. Unbelief whispers, "Let us wait till the obstructions are removed, and we can see our way clearly;" but faith courageously urges an advance, hoping all things, believing all things.

The cloud that was a wall of darkness to the Egyptians was to the Hebrews a great flood of light, illuminating the whole camp, and shedding brightness upon the path before them. So the dealings of Providence bring to the unbelieving, darkness and despair, while to the trusting soul they are full of light and peace. The path where God leads the way may lie through the desert or the sea, but it is a safe path.

Publisher's Note:

In the preceding chapter, we've thrilled to the story of God's miraculous deliverance of His people—a time when He opened a dry path through the Red Sea so they could escape Pharaoh's army. And soon, we'll follow the journey of Israel from the Red Sea through the wilderness of Sinai. But first we leap again across the centuries from Exodus to the book of Revelation—from the past to the future. Because there in Revelation, the Bible's final book, we discover that God will once again deliver His people from their enemies, just prior to the return of Jesus to this earth.

Chapter 6

This chapter is based on selections from throughout the book of Revelation.

Flash Forward: The Deliverance Yet to Come

W hen the protection of human laws shall be withdrawn from those who honor the law of God, there will be, in different lands, a simultaneous movement for their destruction. As the time appointed in the decree draws near, the people will conspire to root out the hated sect. It will be determined to strike in one night a decisive blow, which shall utterly silence the voice of dissent and reproof.

The people of God—some in prison cells, some hidden in solitary retreats in the forests and the mountains—still plead for divine protection, while in every quarter companies of armed men, urged on by hosts of evil angels, are preparing for the work of death. It is now, in the hour of utmost extremity, that the God of Israel will interpose for the deliverance of His chosen. Saith the Lord; "Ye shall have a song, as in the night when a holy solemnity is kept; and gladness of heart, as when one goeth … to come into the mountain of the Lord, to the Mighty One of Israel. And the Lord shall cause His glorious voice to be heard, and shall show the lighting down of His arm, with the indignation of His anger, and with the flame of a devouring fire, with scattering, and tempest, and hailstones." Isaiah 30:29, 30.

With shouts of triumph, jeering, and imprecation, throngs of evil men are about to rush upon their prey, when, lo, a dense blackness, deeper than the darkness of the night, falls upon the earth. Then a rainbow, shining with the glory from the throne of God, spans the heavens and seems to encircle each praying company. The angry multitudes are suddenly arrested. Their mocking cries die away. The objects of their murderous rage are forgotten. With fearful forebodings they gaze upon the symbol of God's covenant and long to be shielded from its overpowering brightness.

By the people of God a voice, clear and melodious, is heard, saying, "Look up," and lifting their eyes to the heavens, they behold the bow of promise. The black, angry clouds that covered the firmament are parted, and like Stephen they look up steadfastly into heaven and see the glory of God and the Son of man seated upon His throne. In His divine form they discern the marks of His humiliation; and from His lips they hear the request presented before His Father and the holy angels: "I will that they also, whom Thou hast given Me, be with Me where I am." John 17:24. Again a voice, musical and triumphant, is heard, saying: "They come! they come! holy, harmless, and undefiled. They have kept the word of My patience; they shall walk among the angels;" and the pale, quivering lips of those who have held fast their faith utter a shout of victory.

Delivered at Midnight

It is at midnight that God manifests His power for the deliverance of His people. The sun appears, shining in its strength. Signs and wonders follow in quick succession. The wicked look with terror and amazement upon the scene, while the righteous behold with solemn joy the tokens of their deliverance. Everything in nature seems turned out of its course. The streams cease to flow. Dark, heavy clouds come up and clash against each other. In the midst of the angry heavens is one clear space of indescribable glory, whence comes the voice of God like the sound of many waters, saying: "It is done." Revelation 16:17.

That voice shakes the heavens and the earth. There is a mighty earthquake, "such as was not since men were upon the earth, so mighty an earthquake, and so great." Verses 17, 18. The firmament appears to open and shut. The glory from the throne of God seems flashing through. The mountains shake like a reed in the wind, and ragged rocks are scattered on every side. There is a roar as of a coming tempest. The sea is lashed into fury. There is heard the shriek of a hurricane like the voice of demons upon a mission of destruction. The whole earth heaves and swells like the waves of the sea. Its surface is breaking up. Its very foundations seem to be giving way. Mountain chains are sinking. Inhabited islands disappear. The seaports that have become like Sodom for wickedness are swallowed up by the angry waters. Babylon the great has come in remembrance before God, "to give unto her the cup of the wine of the fierceness of

His wrath." Great hailstones, every one "about the weight of a talent," are doing their work of destruction. Verses 19, 21. The proudest cities of the earth are laid low. The lordly palaces, upon which the world's great men have lavished their wealth in order to glorify themselves, are crumbling to ruin before their eyes. Prison walls are rent asunder, and God's people, who have been held in bondage for their faith, are set free.

All who have died in the faith of the third angel's message come forth from the tomb glorified.

Graves are opened, and "many of them that sleep in the dust of the earth. … awake, some to everlasting life, and some to shame and everlasting contempt." Daniel 12:2. All who have died in the faith of the third angel's message come forth from the tomb glorified, to hear God's covenant of peace with those who have kept His law. "They also which pierced Him" (Revelation 1:7), those that mocked and derided Christ's dying agonies, and the most violent opposers of His truth and His people, are raised to behold Him in His glory and to see the honor placed upon the loyal and obedient.

Thick clouds still cover the sky; yet the sun now and then breaks through, appearing like the avenging eye of Jehovah. Fierce lightnings leap from the heavens, enveloping the earth in a sheet of flame. Above the terrific roar of thunder, voices, mysterious and awful, declare the doom of the wicked. The words spoken are not comprehended by all; but they are distinctly understood by the false teachers. Those who a little before were so reckless, so boastful and defiant, so exultant in their cruelty to God's commandment-keeping people, are now overwhelmed with consternation and shuddering in fear. Their wails are heard above the sound of the elements. Demons acknowledge the deity of Christ and tremble before His power, while men are supplicating for mercy and groveling in abject terror.

Said the prophets of old, as they beheld in holy vision the day of God: "Howl ye; for the day of the Lord is at hand; it shall come as a destruction from the Almighty." Isaiah 13:6. "Enter into the rock, and hide thee in the dust, for fear of the Lord, and for the glory of His majesty. The lofty looks of man shall be humbled, and the haughtiness of men shall be bowed down, and the Lord alone shall be exalted in that day. For the day of the Lord of hosts shall be upon everyone that is proud and lofty, and upon everyone that is lifted up; and he shall be brought low." "In that day a man shall cast the idols of his silver, and the idols of his gold, which they made each one for himself to worship, to the moles and to the bats; to go into the clefts of the rocks, and into the tops of the ragged rocks, for fear of the Lord, and for the glory of His majesty, when He ariseth to shake terribly the earth." Isaiah 2:10-12, 20, 21, margin.

Through a rift in the clouds there beams a star whose brilliancy is increased fourfold in contrast with the darkness. It speaks hope and joy to the faithful, but severity and wrath to the transgressors of God's law. Those who have sacrificed all for Christ are now secure, hidden as in the secret of the Lord's pavilion. They have been tested, and before the world and the despisers of truth they have evinced their fidelity to Him who died for them. A marvelous change has come over those who have held fast their integrity in the very face of death. They have been suddenly delivered from the dark and terrible tyranny of men transformed to demons.

There appears against the sky a hand holding two tables of stone folded together.

Their faces, so lately pale, anxious, and haggard, are now aglow with wonder, faith, and love. Their voices rise in triumphant song: "God is our refuge and strength, a very present help in trouble. Therefore will not we fear, though the earth be removed, and though the mountains be carried into the midst of the sea; though the waters thereof roar and be troubled, though the mountains shake with the swelling thereof." Psalm 46:1-3.

While these words of holy trust ascend to God, the clouds sweep back, and the starry heavens are seen, unspeakably glorious in contrast with the black and angry firmament on either side. The glory of the celestial city streams from the gates ajar. Then there appears against the sky a hand holding two tables of stone folded together. Says the prophet: "The heavens shall declare His righteousness: for God is judge Himself." Psalm 50:6. That holy law, God's righteousness, that amid thunder and flame was proclaimed from Sinai as the guide of life, is now revealed to men as the rule of judgment. The hand opens the tables, and there are seen the precepts of the Decalogue, traced as with a pen of fire. The words are so plain that all can read them. Memory is aroused, the darkness of superstition and heresy is swept from every mind, and God's ten words, brief, comprehensive, and authoritative, are presented to the view of all the inhabitants of the earth.

It is impossible to describe the horror and despair of those who have trampled upon God's holy requirements. The Lord gave them His law; they might have compared their characters with it and learned their defects while there was yet opportunity for repentance and reform; but in order to secure the favor of the world, they set aside its precepts and taught others to transgress. They have endeavored to compel God's people to profane His Sabbath. Now they are condemned by that law which they have despised. With awful distinctness they see that they are without excuse. They chose whom they would serve and worship. "Then shall ye return, and discern between the righteous and the wicked, between him that serveth God and him that serveth Him not." Malachi 3:18.

Day and Hour of Christ's Coming Announced

The enemies of God's law, from the ministers down to the least among them, have a new conception of truth and duty. Too late they see that the Sabbath of the fourth commandment is the seal of the living God. Too late they see the true nature of their spurious sabbath and the sandy foundation upon which they have been building. They find that they have been fighting against God. Religious teachers have led souls to perdition while professing to guide them to the gates of Paradise. Not until the day of final accounts will it be known how great is the responsibility of men in holy office and how terrible are the results of their unfaithfulness. Only in eternity can we rightly estimate the loss of a single soul. Fearful will be the doom of him to whom God shall say: Depart, thou wicked servant.

The voice of God is heard from heaven, declaring the day and hour of Jesus' coming, and delivering the everlasting covenant to His people. Like peals of loudest thunder His words roll through the earth. The Israel of God stand listening, with their eyes fixed upward. Their countenances are lighted up with His glory, and shine as did the face of Moses when he came down from Sinai. The wicked cannot look upon them. And when the blessing is pronounced on those who have honored God by keeping His Sabbath holy, there is a mighty shout of victory.

Soon there appears in the east a small black cloud, about half the size of a man's hand. It is the cloud which surrounds the Saviour and which seems in the distance to be shrouded in darkness. The people of God know this to be the sign of the Son of man. In solemn silence they gaze upon it as it draws nearer the earth, becoming lighter and more glorious, until it is a great white cloud, its base a glory like consuming fire, and above it the rainbow of the covenant. Jesus rides forth as a mighty conqueror. Not now a "Man of Sorrows," to drink the bitter cup of shame and woe, He comes, victor in heaven and earth, to judge the living and the dead. "Faithful and True," "in righteousness He doth judge and make war." And "the armies which were in heaven" (Revelation 19:11, 14) follow Him. With anthems of celestial melody the holy angels, a vast, unnumbered throng, attend Him on His way. The firmament seems filled with radiant forms—"ten thousand times ten thousand, and thousands of thousands." No human pen can portray the scene; no mortal mind is adequate to conceive its splendor. "His glory covered the heavens, and the earth was full of His praise. And His brightness was as the light." Habakkuk 3:3,4. As the living cloud comes still nearer, every eye beholds the Prince of life. No crown of thorns now mars that sacred head; but a diadem of glory rests on His holy brow. His countenance outshines the dazzling brightness of the noonday sun. "And He hath on His vesture and on His thigh a name written, *King of kings, and Lord of lords.*" Revelation 19:16.

> *There appears in the east a small black cloud, about half the size of a man's hand.*
>
>

Before His presence "all faces are turned into paleness;" upon the rejecters of God's mercy falls the terror of eternal despair. "The heart melteth, and the knees smite together, ... and the faces of them all gather blackness." Jeremiah 30:6; Nahum 2:10. The righteous cry with trembling: "Who shall be able to stand?" The angels' song is hushed, and there is a period of awful silence. Then the voice of Jesus is heard, saying: "My grace is sufficient for you." The faces of the righteous are lighted up, and joy fills every heart. And the angels strike a note higher and sing again as they draw still nearer to the earth.

The King of kings descends upon the cloud, wrapped in flaming fire. The heavens are rolled together as a scroll, the earth trembles before Him, and every mountain and island is moved out of its place. "Our God shall come, and shall not keep silence: a fire shall devour before Him, and it shall be very tempestuous round about Him. He shall call to the heavens from above, and to the earth, that He may judge His people." Psalm 50:3, 4.

The wicked pray to be buried beneath the rocks of the mountains.

And the kings of the earth, and the great men, and the rich men, and the chief captains, and the mighty men, and every bondman, and every freeman, hid themselves in the dens and in the rocks of the mountains; and said to the mountains and rocks, Fall on us, and hide us from the face of Him that sitteth on the throne, and from the wrath of the Lamb: for the great day of His wrath is come; and who shall be able to stand? Revelation 6:15–17

The derisive jests have ceased. Lying lips are hushed into silence. The clash of arms, the tumult of battle, "with confused noise, and garments rolled in blood" (Isaiah 9:5), is stilled. Nought now is heard but the voice of prayer and the sound of weeping and lamentation. The cry bursts forth from lips so lately scoffing: "The great day of His wrath is come; and who shall be able to stand?" The wicked pray to be buried beneath the rocks of the mountains rather than meet the face of Him whom they have despised and rejected.

That voice which penetrates the ear of the dead, they know. How often have its plaintive, tender tones called them to repentance. How often has it been heard in the touching entreaties of a friend, a brother, a Redeemer. To the rejecters of His grace no other could be so full of condemnation, so burdened with denunciation, as that voice which has so long pleaded: "Turn ye, turn ye from your evil ways; for why will ye die?" Ezekiel 33:11. Oh, that it were to them the voice of a stranger! Says Jesus: "I have called, and ye refused; I have stretched out My hand, and no man regarded; but ye have set at nought all My counsel, and would none of My reproof." Proverbs 1:24, 25. That voice awakens memories which they would fain blot out—warnings despised, invitations refused, privileges slighted.

There are those who mocked Christ in His humiliation. With thrilling power come to their minds the Sufferer's words, when, adjured by the high priest, He solemnly declared: "Hereafter shall ye see the Son of man sitting on the right hand of power, and coming in the clouds of heaven." Matthew 26:64. Now they behold Him in His glory, and they are yet to see Him sitting on the right hand of power.

Now they behold Him in His glory, and they are yet to see Him sitting on the right hand of power.

Those who derided His claim to be the Son of God are speechless now. There is the haughty Herod who jeered at His royal title and bade the mocking soldiers crown Him king. There are the very men who with impious hands placed upon His form the purple robe, upon His sacred brow the thorny crown, and in His unresisting hand the mimic scepter, and bowed before Him in blasphemous mockery. The men who smote and spit upon the Prince of life now turn from His piercing gaze and seek to flee from the overpowering glory of His presence. Those who drove the nails through His hands and feet, the soldier who pierced His side, behold these marks with terror and remorse.

With awful distinctness do priests and rulers recall the events of Calvary. With shuddering horror they remember how, wagging their heads in satanic exultation, they exclaimed: "He saved others; Himself He cannot save. If He be the King of Israel, let Him now come down from the cross, and we will believe Him. He trusted in God; let Him deliver Him now, if He will have Him." Matthew 27:42, 43.

Vividly they recall the Saviour's parable of the husbandmen who refused to render to their lord the fruit of the vineyard, who abused his servants and slew his son. They remember, too, the sentence which they themselves pronounced: The lord of the vineyard "will miserably destroy those wicked men." In the sin and punishment of those unfaithful men the priests and elders see their own course and their own just doom. And now there rises a cry of mortal agony. Louder than the shout, "Crucify Him, crucify Him," which rang through the streets of Jerusalem, swells the awful, despairing wail, "He is the Son of God! He is the true Messiah!" They seek to flee from the presence of the King of kings. In the deep caverns of the earth, rent asunder by the warring of the elements, they vainly attempt to hide.

In the lives of all who reject truth there are moments when conscience awakens, when memory presents the torturing recollection of a life of hypocrisy and the soul is harassed with vain regrets. But what are these compared with the remorse of that day when "fear cometh as desolation," when "destruction cometh as a whirlwind"! Proverbs 1:27. Those who would have destroyed Christ and His faithful people now witness the glory which rests upon them. In the midst of their terror they hear the voices of the saints in joyful strains exclaiming: "Lo, this is our God; we have waited for Him, and He will save us." Isaiah 25:9.

Amid the reeling of the earth, the flash of lightning, and the roar of thunder, the voice of the Son of God calls forth the sleeping saints. He looks upon the graves of the righteous, then, raising His hands to heaven, He cries: "Awake, awake, awake, ye that sleep in the dust, and arise!" Throughout the length and breadth of the earth the dead shall hear that voice, and they that hear shall live. And the whole earth shall ring with the tread of the exceeding great army of every nation, kindred, tongue, and people.

The voice of the Son of God calls forth the sleeping saints. ... From the prison house of death they come.

From the prison house of death they come, clothed with immortal glory, crying: "O death, where is thy sting? O grave, where is thy victory?" 1 Corinthians 15:55. And the living righteous and the risen saints unite their voices in a long, glad shout of victory.

All come forth from their graves the same in stature as when they entered the tomb. Adam, who stands among the risen throng, is of lofty height and majestic form, in stature but little below the Son of God. He presents a marked contrast to the people of later generations; in this one respect is shown the great degeneracy of the race. But all arise with the freshness and vigor of eternal youth. In the beginning, man was created in the likeness of God, not only in character, but in form and feature. Sin defaced and almost obliterated the divine image; but Christ came to restore that which had been lost. He will change our vile bodies and fashion them like unto His glorious body. The mortal, corruptible form, devoid of comeliness, once polluted with sin, becomes perfect, beautiful, and immortal. All blemishes and deformities are left in the grave. Restored to the tree of life in the long-lost Eden, the redeemed will "grow up" (Malachi 4:2) to the full stature of the race in its primeval glory. The last lingering traces of the curse of sin will be removed, and Christ's faithful ones will appear in "the beauty of the Lord our God," in mind and soul and body reflecting the perfect image of their Lord. Oh, wonderful redemption! long talked of, long hoped for, contemplated with eager anticipation, but never fully understood.

The living righteous are changed "in a moment, in the twinkling of an eye." At the voice of God they were glorified; now they are made immortal and with the risen saints are caught up to meet their Lord in the air. Angels "gather together His elect from the four winds, from one end of heaven to the other." Little children are borne by holy angels to their mothers' arms. Friends long separated by death are united, nevermore to part, and with songs of gladness ascend together to the City of God.

A Cloudy, Heaven-Bound Chariot

On each side of the cloudy chariot are wings, and beneath it are living wheels; and as the chariot rolls upward, the wheels cry, "Holy," and the wings, as they move, cry, "Holy," and the retinue of angels cry, "Holy, holy, holy, Lord God Almighty." And the redeemed shout, "Alleluia!" as the chariot moves onward toward the New Jerusalem.

Before entering the City of God, the Saviour bestows upon His followers the emblems of victory and invests them with the insignia of their royal state. The glittering ranks are drawn up in the form of a hollow square about their King, whose form rises in majesty high above saint and angel, whose countenance beams upon them full of benignant love. Throughout the unnumbered host of the redeemed every glance is fixed upon Him, every eye beholds His glory whose "visage was so marred more than any man, and His form more than the sons of men." Upon the heads of the overcomers, Jesus with His own right hand places the crown of glory. For each there is a crown, bearing his own "new name" (Revelation 2:17), and the inscription, "Holiness to the Lord." In every hand are placed the victor's palm and the shining harp. Then, as the commanding angels strike the note, every hand sweeps the harp strings with skillful touch, awaking sweet music in rich, melodious strains. Rapture unutterable thrills every heart, and each voice is raised in grateful praise: "Unto Him that loved us, and washed us from our sins in His own blood, and hath made us kings and priests unto God and His Father; to Him be glory and dominion for ever and ever." Revelation 1:5,6.

Before the ransomed throng is the Holy City. Jesus opens wide the pearly gates, and the nations that have kept the truth enter in. There they behold the Paradise of God, the home of Adam in his innocency. Then that voice, richer than any music that ever fell on mortal ear, is heard, saying: "Your conflict is ended." "Come, ye blessed of My Father, inherit the kingdom prepared for you from the foundation of the world."

With unutterable love, Jesus welcomes His faithful ones to the joy of their Lord.

Now is fulfilled the Saviour's prayer for His disciples: "I will that they also, whom Thou hast given Me, be with Me where I am." "Faultless before the presence of His glory with exceeding joy" (Jude 24), Christ presents to the Father the purchase of His blood, declaring: "Here am I, and the children whom Thou hast given Me." "Those that Thou gavest Me I have kept." Oh, the wonders of redeeming love! the rapture of that hour when the infinite Father, looking upon the ransomed, shall behold His image, sin's discord banished, its blight removed, and the human once more in harmony with the divine!

With unutterable love, Jesus welcomes His faithful ones to the joy of their Lord. The Saviour's joy is in seeing, in the kingdom of glory, the souls that have been saved by His agony and humiliation. And the redeemed will be sharers in His joy, as they behold, among the blessed, those who have been won to Christ through their prayers, their labors, and their loving sacrifice. As they gather about the great white throne, gladness unspeakable will fill their hearts, when they behold those whom they have won for Christ, and see that one has gained others, and these still others, all brought into the haven of rest, there to lay their crowns at Jesus' feet and praise Him through the endless cycles of eternity.

The Two Adams Meet

As the ransomed ones are welcomed to the City of God, there rings out upon the air an exultant cry of adoration. The two Adams are about to meet. The Son of God is standing with outstretched arms to receive the father of our race—the being whom He created, who sinned against his Maker, and for whose sin the marks of the crucifixion are borne upon the Saviour's form. As Adam discerns the prints of the cruel nails, he does not fall upon the bosom of his Lord, but in humiliation casts himself at His feet, crying: "Worthy, worthy is the Lamb that was slain!" Tenderly the Saviour lifts him up and bids him look once more upon the Eden home from which he has so long been exiled.

After his expulsion from Eden, Adam's life on earth was filled with sorrow. Every dying leaf, every victim of sacrifice, every blight upon the fair face of nature, every stain upon man's purity, was a fresh reminder of his sin. Terrible was the agony of remorse as he beheld iniquity abounding, and, in answer to his warnings, met the reproaches cast upon himself as the cause of sin. With patient humility he bore, for nearly a thousand years, the penalty of transgression. Faithfully did he repent of his sin and trust in the merits of the promised Saviour, and he died in the hope of a resurrection. The Son of God redeemed man's failure and fall; and now, through the work of the atonement, Adam is reinstated in his first dominion.

Transported with joy, he beholds the trees that were once his delight—the very trees whose fruit he himself had gathered in the days of his innocence and joy. He sees the vines that his own hands have trained, the very flowers that he once loved to care for. His mind grasps the reality of the scene; he comprehends that this is indeed Eden restored, more lovely now than when he was banished from it. The Saviour leads him to the tree of life and plucks the glorious fruit and bids him eat. He looks about him and beholds a multitude of his family redeemed, standing in the Paradise of God. Then he casts his glittering crown at the feet of Jesus and, falling upon His breast, embraces the Redeemer. He touches the golden harp, and the vaults of heaven echo the triumphant song: "Worthy, worthy, worthy is the Lamb that was slain, and lives again!" The family of Adam take up the strain and cast their crowns at the Saviour's feet as they bow before Him in adoration.

This reunion is witnessed by the angels who wept at the fall of Adam and rejoiced when Jesus, after His resurrection, ascended to heaven, having opened the grave for all who should believe on His name. Now they behold the work of redemption accomplished, and they unite their voices in the song of praise.

The Sea of Glass Before the Throne

Upon the crystal sea before the throne, that sea of glass as it were mingled with fire,—so resplendent is it with the glory of God,—are gathered the company that have "gotten the victory over the beast, and over his image, and over his mark, and over the number of his name." With the Lamb upon Mount Zion, "having the harps of God," they stand, the hundred and forty and four thousand that were redeemed from among men; and there is heard, as the sound of many waters, and as the sound of a great thunder, "the voice of harpers harping with their harps." And they sing "a new song" before the throne, a song which no man can learn save the hundred and forty and four thousand. It is the song of Moses and the Lamb—a song of deliverance. None but the hundred and forty-four thousand can learn that song; for it is the song of their experience—an experience such as no other company have ever had. "These are they which follow the Lamb whithersoever He goeth." These, having been translated from the earth, from among the living, are counted as "the first fruits unto God and to the Lamb." Revelation 15:2, 3; 14:1-5. "These are they which came out of great tribulation;" they have passed through the time of trouble such as never was since there was a nation; they have endured the anguish of the time of Jacob's trouble; they have stood without an intercessor through the final outpouring of God's judgments. But they have been delivered, for they have "washed their robes, and made them white in the blood of the Lamb." "In their mouth was found no guile: for they are without fault" before God. "Therefore are they before the throne of God, and serve Him day and night in His temple: and He that sitteth on the throne shall dwell among them." They have seen the earth wasted with famine and pestilence, the sun having power to scorch men with great heat, and they themselves have endured suffering, hunger, and thirst. But "they shall hunger no more, neither thirst any more; neither shall the sun light on them, nor any heat. For the Lamb which is in the midst of the throne shall feed them, and shall lead them unto living fountains of waters: and God shall wipe away all tears from their eyes." Revelation 7:14-17.

In all ages the Saviour's chosen have been educated and disciplined in the school of trial. They walked in narrow paths on earth;

they were purified in the furnace of affliction. For Jesus' sake they endured opposition, hatred, calumny. They followed Him through conflicts sore; they endured self-denial and experienced bitter disappointments. By their own painful experience they learned the evil of sin, its power, its guilt, its woe; and they look upon it with abhorrence. A sense of the infinite sacrifice made for its cure humbles them in their own sight and fills their hearts with gratitude and praise which those who have never fallen cannot appreciate. They love much because they have been forgiven much. Having been partakers of Christ's sufferings, they are fitted to be partakers with Him of His glory.

The heirs of God have come from garrets, from hovels, from dungeons, from scaffolds, from mountains, from deserts, from the caves of the earth, from the caverns of the sea. On earth they were "destitute, afflicted, tormented." Millions went down to the grave loaded with infamy because they steadfastly refused to yield to the deceptive claims of Satan. By human tribunals they were adjudged the vilest of criminals. But now "God is judge Himself." Psalm 50:6. Now the decisions of earth are reversed. "The rebuke of His people shall He take away." Isaiah 25:8. "They shall call them, The holy people, The redeemed of the Lord." He hath appointed "to give unto them beauty for ashes, the oil of joy for mourning, the garment of praise for the spirit of heaviness." Isaiah 62:12; 61:3. They are no longer feeble, afflicted, scattered, and oppressed. Henceforth they are to be ever with the Lord. They stand before the throne clad in richer robes than the most honored of the earth have ever worn. They are crowned with diadems more glorious than were ever placed upon the brow of earthly monarchs. The days of pain and weeping are forever ended. The King of glory has wiped the tears from all faces; every cause of grief has been removed. Amid the waving of palm branches they pour forth a song of praise, clear, sweet, and harmonious; every voice takes up the strain, until the anthem swells through the vaults of heaven: "Salvation to our God which sitteth upon the throne, and unto the Lamb." And all the inhabitants of heaven respond in the ascription: "Amen: Blessing, and glory, and wisdom, and thanksgiving, and honor, and power, and might, be unto our God for ever and ever." Revelation 7:10, 12.

> *They love much because they have been forgiven much.*

In this life we can only begin to understand the wonderful theme of redemption. With our finite comprehension we may consider most earnestly the shame and the glory, the life and the death, the justice and the mercy, that meet in the cross; yet with the utmost stretch of our mental powers we fail to grasp its full significance. The length and the breadth, the depth and the height, of redeeming love are but dimly comprehended. The plan of redemption will not be fully understood, even when the ransomed see as they are seen and know as they are known; but through the eternal ages new truth will continually unfold to the wondering and delighted mind. Though the griefs and pains and temptations of earth are ended and the cause removed, the people of God will ever have a distinct, intelligent knowledge of what their salvation has cost.

The Cross of Christ Our Eternal Science and Song

The cross of Christ will be the science and the song of the redeemed through all eternity. In Christ glorified they will behold Christ crucified. Never will it be forgotten that He whose power created and upheld the unnumbered worlds through the vast realms of space, the Beloved of God, the Majesty of heaven, He whom cherub and shining seraph delighted to adore—humbled Himself to uplift fallen man; that He bore the guilt and shame of sin, and the hiding of His Father's face, till the woes of a lost world broke His heart and crushed out His life on Calvary's cross. That the Maker of all worlds, the Arbiter of all destinies, should lay aside His glory and humiliate Himself from love to man will ever excite the wonder and adoration of the universe. As the nations of the saved look upon their Redeemer and behold the eternal glory of the Father shining in His countenance; as they behold His throne, which is from everlasting to everlasting, and know that His kingdom is to have no end, they break forth in rapturous song: "Worthy, worthy is the Lamb that was slain, and hath redeemed us to God by His own most precious blood!"

The mystery of the cross explains all other mysteries. In the light that streams from Calvary the attributes of God which had filled us with fear and awe appear beautiful and attractive. Mercy, tenderness, and parental love are seen to blend with holiness, justice, and power. While we behold the majesty of His throne, high and lifted up, we see His character in its gracious manifestations, and comprehend, as never before, the significance of that endearing title, "Our Father."

It will be seen that He who is infinite in wisdom could devise no plan for our salvation except the sacrifice of His Son. The compensation for this sacrifice is the joy of peopling the earth with ransomed beings, holy, happy, and immortal. The result of the Saviour's conflict with the powers of darkness is joy to the redeemed, redounding to the glory of God throughout eternity. And such is the value of the soul that the Father is satisfied with the price paid; and Christ Himself, beholding the fruits of His great sacrifice, is satisfied.

Part 3

From the Exodus Toward the Promised Land

From the Song of Moses...

I will sing to the Lord,

For He has triumphed gloriously!

The horse and its rider

He has thrown into the sea!

The Lord is my strength and song,

And He has become my salvation;

He is my God, and I will praise Him;

My father's God, and I will exalt Him.

The Lord is a man of war;

The Lord is His name.

Pharaoh's chariots and his army He has cast
*   into the sea;*
His chosen captains also are drowned in the Red Sea.

The depths have covered them;

They sank to the bottom like a stone.

—*Exodus 15:1–5*

Part 3

Thought Questions

- Almost immediately after the great deliverance of the Exodus, as the Israelites made their way through the wilderness of Sinai, they began complaining and doubting God. We learn of this and shake our heads at their lack of faith. But have we ever come to a difficult place in life and almost totally forgotten all that God has done for us in the past?

- On Mount Sinai, God gave Moses the Ten Commandment law. Moses in turn brought it to the Israelites. But God's purpose was not just to bring it TO them but rather, that the law would be shared THROUGH them with all other nations. Do you believe that this is still God's plan for His people today?

- When Moses came down from Mount Sinai, Israel had swiftly fallen into apostasy and idol worship. This was largely due to the desire of Aaron, Moses' brother, to please the Israelites. Is not this experience a strong warning to us of the dangers of people-pleasing?

Chapter 7

This chapter is based on Exodus 15:22–27; 16–18.

From the Red Sea to Mount Sinai

From the Red Sea the hosts of Israel again set forth on their journey, under the guidance of the pillar of cloud. The scene around them was most dreary—bare, desolate-looking mountains, barren plains, and the sea stretching far away, its shores strewn with the bodies of their enemies; yet they were full of joy in the consciousness of freedom, and every thought of discontent was hushed.

But for three days, as they journeyed, they could find no water. The supply which they had taken with them was exhausted. There was nothing to quench their burning thirst as they dragged wearily over the sun-burnt plains. Moses, who was familiar with this region, knew what the others did not, that at Marah, the nearest station where springs were to be found, the water was unfit for use. With intense anxiety he watched the guiding cloud. With a sinking heart he heard the glad shout, "Water! water!" echoed along the line. Men, women, and children in joyous haste crowded to the fountain, when, lo, a cry of anguish burst forth from the host—the water was bitter.

In their horror and despair they reproached Moses for having led them in such a way, not remembering that the divine presence in that mysterious cloud had been leading him as well as them. In his grief at their distress Moses did what they had forgotten to do; he cried earnestly to God for help. "And the Lord showed him a tree, which when he had cast into the waters, the waters were made sweet." Here the promise was given to Israel through Moses, "If thou wilt diligently hearken to the voice of the Lord thy God, and wilt do that which is right in His sight, and wilt give ear to His commandments, and keep all His statutes, I will put none of these diseases upon thee, which I have brought upon the Egyptians: for I am the Lord that healeth thee."

From Marah the people journeyed to Elim, where they found "twelve wells of water, and threescore and ten palm trees." Here they remained several days before entering the wilderness of Sin. When they had been a month absent from Egypt, they made their first encampment in the wilderness. Their store of provisions had now begun to fail. There was scanty herbage in the wilderness, and their flocks were diminishing. How was food to be supplied for these vast multitudes? Doubts filled their hearts, and again they murmured. Even the rulers and elders of the people joined in complaining against the leaders of God's appointment: "Would to God we had died by the hand of the Lord in the land of Egypt, when we sat by the fleshpots, and when we did eat bread to the full; for ye have brought us forth into this wilderness, to kill this whole assembly with hunger."

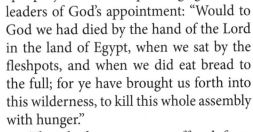

If in their want they would call upon Him, He would still grant them manifest tokens of His love and care.

They had not as yet suffered from hunger; their present wants were supplied, but they feared for the future. They could not understand how these vast multitudes were to subsist in their travels through the wilderness, and in imagination they saw their children famishing. The Lord permitted difficulties to surround them, and their supply of food to be cut short, that their hearts might turn to Him who had hitherto been their Deliverer. If in their want they would call upon Him, He would still grant them manifest tokens of His love and care. He had promised that if they would obey His commandments, no disease should come upon them, and it was sinful unbelief on their part to anticipate that they or their children might die of hunger.

God had promised to be their God, to take them to Himself as a people, and to lead them to a large and good land; but they were ready to faint at every obstacle encountered in the way to that land. In a marvelous manner He had brought them out from their bondage in Egypt, that He might elevate and ennoble them and make them a praise in the earth. But it was necessary for them to encounter difficulties and to endure privations. God was bringing them from a state of degradation and fitting them to occupy an honorable place among the nations and to receive important and sacred trusts. Had they possessed faith in Him, in view of all that He had wrought for them, they would cheerfully have borne inconvenience, privation, and even real suffering; but they were unwilling to trust the Lord any further than they could witness the continual evidences of His power. They forgot their bitter service in Egypt. They forgot the goodness and power of God displayed in their behalf in their deliverance from bondage. They forgot how their children had been spared when the destroying angel slew all the first-born of Egypt. They forgot the grand exhibition of divine power at the Red Sea. They forgot that while they had crossed safely in the path that had been opened for them, the armies of their enemies, attempting to follow them, had been overwhelmed by the waters of the sea. They saw and felt only their present inconveniences and trials; and instead of saying, "God has done great things for us; whereas we were slaves, He is making of us a great nation," they talked of the hardness of the way, and wondered when their weary pilgrimage would end.

The history of the wilderness life of Israel was chronicled for the benefit of the Israel of God to the close of time. The record of God's dealings with the wanderers of the desert in all their marchings to and fro, in their exposure to hunger, thirst, and weariness, and in the striking manifestations of His power for their relief, is fraught with warning and instruction for His people in all ages. The varied experience of the Hebrews was a school of preparation for their promised home in Canaan. God would have His people in these days review with a humble heart and teachable spirit the trials through which ancient Israel passed, that they may be instructed in their preparation for the heavenly Canaan.

Though their present needs are supplied, many are unwilling to trust God for the future.

Many look back to the Israelites, and marvel at their unbelief and murmuring, feeling that they themselves would not have been so ungrateful; but when their faith is tested, even by little trials, they manifest no more faith or patience than did ancient Israel. When brought into strait places, they murmur at the process by which God has chosen to purify them. Though their present needs are supplied, many are unwilling to trust God for the future, and they are in constant anxiety lest poverty shall come upon them, and their children shall be left to suffer. Some are always anticipating evil or magnifying the difficulties that really exist, so that their eyes are blinded to the many blessings which demand their gratitude. The obstacles they encounter, instead of leading them to seek help from God, the only Source of strength, separate them from Him, because they awaken unrest and repining.

Do we well to be thus unbelieving? Why should we be ungrateful and distrustful? Jesus is our friend; all heaven is interested in our welfare; and our anxiety and fear grieve the Holy Spirit of God. We should not indulge in a solicitude that only frets and wears us, but does not help us to bear trials. No place should be given to that distrust of God which leads us to make a preparation against future want the chief pursuit of life, as though our happiness consisted in these earthly things. It is not the will of God that His people should be weighed down with care. But our Lord does not tell us that there are no dangers in our path. He does not propose to take His people out of the world of sin and evil, but He points us to a never-failing refuge. He invites the weary and care-laden, "Come unto Me, all ye that labor and are heavy-laden, and I will give you rest." Lay off the yoke of anxiety and worldly care that you have placed on your own neck, and "take My yoke upon you, and learn of Me; for I am meek and lowly in heart: and ye shall find rest unto your souls." Matthew 11:28, 29. We may find rest and peace in God, casting all our care upon Him; for He careth for us. See 1 Peter 5:7.

> *It is not the will of God that His people should be weighed down with care.*

Says the apostle Paul, "Take heed, brethren, lest there be in any of you an evil heart of unbelief, in departing from the living God." Hebrews 3:12. In view of all that God has wrought for us, our faith should be strong, active, and enduring. Instead of murmuring and complaining, the language of our hearts should be, "Bless the Lord, O my soul: and all that is within me, bless His holy name. Bless the Lord, O my soul, and forget not all His benefits." Psalm 103:1, 2.

God was not unmindful of the wants of Israel. He said to their leader, "I will rain bread from heaven for you." And directions were given that the people gather a daily supply, with a double amount on the sixth day, that the sacred observance of the Sabbath might be maintained.

Moses assured the congregation that their wants were to be supplied: "The Lord shall give you in the evening flesh to eat, and in the morning bread to the full." And he added, "What are we? your murmurings are not against us, but against the Lord." He further bade Aaron say to them, "Come near before the Lord: for He hath heard your murmurings." While Aaron was speaking, "they looked toward the wilderness, and, behold, the glory of the Lord appeared in the cloud." A splendor such as they had never witnessed symbolized the divine Presence. Through manifestations addressed to their senses, they were to obtain a knowledge of God. They must be taught that the Most High, and not merely the man Moses, was their leader, that they might fear His name and obey His voice.

At nightfall the camp was surrounded by vast flocks of quails, enough to supply the entire company. In the morning there lay upon the surface of the ground "a small round thing, as small as the hoarfrost." "It was like coriander seed, white." The people called it "manna." Moses said, "This is the bread which the Lord hath given you to eat." The people gathered the manna, and found that there was an abundant supply for all. They "ground it in mills, or beat it in a mortar, and baked it in pans, and made cakes of it." Numbers 11:8. "And the taste of it was like wafers made with honey." They were directed to gather daily an omer for every person; and they were not to leave of it until the morning. Some attempted to keep a supply until the next day, but it was then found to be unfit for food. The provision for the day must be gathered in the morning; for all that remained upon the ground was melted by the sun.

Some attempted to keep a supply until the next day, but it was then found to be unfit for food.

In the gathering of the manna it was found that some obtained more and some less than the stipulated amount; but "when they did mete it with an omer, he that gathered much had nothing over, and he that gathered little had no lack." An explanation of this scripture, as well as a practical lesson from it, is given by the apostle Paul in his second epistle to the Corinthians. He says, "I mean not that other men be eased, and ye burdened: but by an equality, that now at this time your abundance may be a supply for their want, that their abundance also may be a supply for your want: that there may be equality: as it is written, He that had gathered much had nothing over; and he that had gathered little had no lack." 2 Corinthians 8:13-15.

On the sixth day the people gathered two omers for every person. The rulers hastened to acquaint Moses with what had been done. His answer was, "This is that which the Lord hath said, Tomorrow is the rest of the holy Sabbath unto the Lord: bake that which ye will bake today, and seethe that ye will seethe; and that which remaineth over lay up for you to be kept until the morning." They did so, and found that it remained unchanged. "And Moses said, Eat that today; for today is a Sabbath unto the Lord: today ye shall not find it in the field. Six days ye shall gather it; but on the seventh day, which is the Sabbath, in it there shall be none."

The Sabbath Command Still to Be Observed

God requires that His holy day be as sacredly observed now as in the time of Israel. The command given to the Hebrews should be regarded by all Christians as an injunction from Jehovah to them. The day before the Sabbath should be made a day of preparation, that everything may be in readiness for its sacred hours. In no case should our own business be allowed to encroach upon holy time. God has directed that the sick and suffering be cared for; the labor required to make them comfortable is a work of mercy, and no violation of the Sabbath; but all unnecessary work should be avoided. Many carelessly put off till the beginning of the Sabbath little things that might have been done on the day of preparation. This should not be. Work that is neglected until the beginning of the Sabbath should remain undone until it is past. This course might help the memory of these thoughtless ones, and make them careful to do their own work on the six working days.

Every week during their long sojourn in the wilderness the Israelites witnessed a threefold miracle, designed to impress their minds with the sacredness of the Sabbath: a double quantity of manna fell on the sixth day, none on the seventh, and the portion needed for the Sabbath was preserved sweet and pure, when if any were kept over at any other time it became unfit for use.

In the circumstances connected with the giving of the manna, we have conclusive evidence that the Sabbath was not instituted, as many claim, when the law was given at Sinai. Before the Israelites came to Sinai they understood the Sabbath to be obligatory upon them. In being obliged to gather every Friday a double portion of manna in preparation for the Sabbath, when none would fall, the sacred nature of the day of rest was continually impressed upon them. And when some of the people went out on the Sabbath to gather manna, the Lord asked, "How long *refuse ye* to keep My commandments and My laws?"

"The children of Israel did eat manna forty years, until they came to a land inhabited: they did eat manna, until they came unto the borders of the land of Canaan." For forty years they were daily reminded by this miraculous provision, of God's unfailing care and tender love. In the words of the psalmist, God gave them "of the corn of heaven. Man did eat angels' food" (Psalm 78:24, 25)—that is,

The manna was a type of Him who came from God to give life to the world.

food provided for them by the angels. Sustained by "the corn of heaven," they were daily taught that, having God's promise, they were as secure from want as if surrounded by fields of waving grain on the fertile plains of Canaan.

The manna, falling from heaven for the sustenance of Israel, was a type of Him who came from God to give life to the world. Said Jesus, "I am that Bread of life. Your fathers did eat manna in the wilderness, and are dead. This is the bread which cometh down from heaven. ...If any man eat of this bread, he shall live forever: and the bread that I will give is My flesh, which I will give for the life of the world." John 6:48-51. And among the promises of blessing to God's people in the future life it is written, "To him that overcometh will I give to eat of the hidden manna." Revelation 2:17.

After leaving the wilderness of Sin, the Israelites encamped in Rephidim. Here there was no water, and again they distrusted the providence of God. In their blindness and presumption the people came to Moses with the demand, "Give us water that we may drink." But his patience failed not. "Why chide ye with me?" he said; "wherefore do ye tempt the Lord?" They cried in anger, "Wherefore is this, that thou hast brought us up out of Egypt, to kill us and our children and our cattle with thirst?" When they had been so abundantly supplied with food, they remembered with shame their unbelief and murmurings, and promised to trust the Lord in the future; but they soon forgot their promise, and failed at the first trial of their faith.

The pillar of cloud that was leading them seemed to veil a fearful mystery. And Moses—who was he? they questioned, and what could be his object in bringing them from Egypt? Suspicion and distrust filled their hearts, and they boldly accused him of designing to kill them and their children by privations and hardships that he might enrich himself with their possessions. In the tumult of rage and indignation they were about to stone him.

In distress Moses cried to the Lord, "What shall I do unto this people?" He was directed to take the elders of Israel and the rod wherewith he had wrought wonders in Egypt, and to go on before the people. And the Lord said unto him, "Behold, I will stand before thee there upon the rock in Horeb; and thou shalt smite the rock, and there shall come water out of it, that the people may drink." He obeyed, and the waters burst forth in a living stream that abundantly supplied the encampment. Instead of commanding Moses to lift up his rod and call down some terrible plague, like those on Egypt, upon the leaders in this wicked murmuring, the Lord in His great mercy made the rod His instrument to work their deliverance.

"He clave the rocks in the wilderness, and gave them drink as out of the great depths. He brought streams also out of the rock, and caused waters to run down like rivers." Psalm 78:15, 16. Moses smote the rock, but it was the Son of God who, veiled in the cloudy pillar, stood beside Moses, and caused the life-giving water to flow. Not only Moses and the elders, but all the congregation who stood at a distance, beheld the glory of the Lord; but had the cloud been removed, they would have been slain by the terrible brightness of Him who abode therein.

In their thirst the people had tempted God, saying, "Is the Lord among us, or not?"—"If God has brought us here, why does He not give us water as well as bread?" The unbelief thus manifested was criminal, and Moses feared that the judgments of God would rest upon them. And he called the name of the place Massah, "temptation," and Meribah, "chiding," as a memorial of their sin.

A new danger now threatened them. Because of their murmuring against Him, the Lord suffered them to be attacked by their enemies. The Amalekites, a fierce, warlike tribe inhabiting that region, came out against them and smote those who, faint and weary, had fallen into the rear. Moses, knowing that the masses of the people were unprepared for battle, directed Joshua to choose from the different tribes a body of soldiers, and lead them on the morrow against the enemy, while he himself would stand on an eminence near by with the rod of God in his hand. Accordingly the next day Joshua and his company attacked the foe, while Moses and Aaron and Hur were stationed on a hill overlooking the battlefield. With arms outstretched toward heaven, and holding the rod of God in his right hand, Moses prayed for the success of the armies of Israel. As the battle progressed, it was observed that so long as his hands were reaching upward, Israel prevailed, but when they were lowered, the enemy was victorious. As Moses became weary, Aaron and Hur stayed up his hands until the going down of the sun, when the enemy was put to flight.

The Duty of Upholding Our Spiritual Leaders

As Aaron and Hur supported the hands of Moses, they showed the people their duty to sustain him in his arduous work while he should receive the word from God to speak to them. And the act of Moses also was significant, showing that God held their destiny in His hands; while they made Him their trust, He would fight for them and subdue their enemies; but when they should let go their hold upon Him, and trust in their own power, they would be even weaker than those who had not the knowledge of God, and their foes would prevail against them.

As the Hebrews triumphed when Moses was reaching his hands toward heaven and interceding in their behalf, so the Israel of God prevail when they by faith take hold upon the strength of their mighty Helper. Yet divine strength is to be combined with human effort. Moses did not believe that God would overcome their foes while Israel remained inactive. While the great leader was pleading with the Lord, Joshua and his brave followers were putting forth their utmost efforts to repulse the enemies of Israel and of God.

After the defeat of the Amalekites, God directed Moses, "Write this for a memorial in a book, and rehearse it in the ears of Joshua: for I will utterly put out the remembrance of Amalek from under heaven." Just before his death the great leader delivered to his people the solemn charge: "Remember what Amalek did unto thee by the way, when ye were come forth out of Egypt; how he met thee by the way, and smote the hindmost of thee, even all that were feeble behind thee, when thou wast faint and weary; and he feared not God. ... Thou shalt blot out the remembrance of Amalek from under heaven; thou shalt not forget it." Deuteronomy 25:17-19. Concerning this wicked people the Lord declared, "The hand of Amalek is against the throne of Jehovah." Exodus 17:16, margin.

The Amalekites were not ignorant of God's character or of His sovereignty, but instead of fearing before Him, they had set themselves to defy His power. The wonders wrought by Moses before the Egyptians were made a subject of mockery by the people of Amalek, and the fears of surrounding nations were ridiculed. They had taken oath by their gods that they would destroy the Hebrews, so that not one should escape, and they boasted that Israel's God would be powerless to resist them. They had not been injured or threatened by the Israelites. Their assault was wholly unprovoked. It was to manifest their hatred and defiance of God that they sought to destroy His people. The Amalekites had long been high-handed sinners, and their crimes had cried to God for vengeance, yet His mercy had still called them to repentance; but when the men of Amalek fell upon the wearied and defenseless ranks of Israel, they sealed their nation's doom. The care of God is over the weakest of His children. No act of cruelty or oppression toward them is unmarked by Heaven. Over all who love and fear Him, His hand extends as a shield; let men beware that they smite not that hand; for it wields the sword of justice.

The care of God is over the weakest of His children.

Not far distant from where the Israelites were now encamped was the home of Jethro, the father-in-law of Moses. Jethro had heard of the deliverance of the Hebrews, and he now set out to visit them, and restore to Moses his wife and two sons. The great leader was informed by messengers of their approach, and he went out with joy to meet them, and, the first greetings over, conducted them to his tent. He had sent back his family when on his way to the perils of leading Israel from Egypt, but now he could again enjoy the relief and comfort of their society. To Jethro he recounted the wonderful dealings of God with Israel, and the patriarch rejoiced and blessed the Lord, and with Moses and the elders he united in offering sacrifice and holding a solemn feast in commemoration of God's mercy.

As Jethro remained in the camp, he soon saw how heavy were the burdens that rested upon Moses. To maintain order and discipline among that vast, ignorant, and untrained multitude was indeed a stupendous task. Moses was their recognized leader and magistrate, and not only the general interests and duties of the people, but the controversies that arose among them, were referred to him. He had permitted this, for it gave him an opportunity to instruct them; as he said, "I do make them know the statutes of God, and His laws." But Jethro remonstrated against this, saying, "This thing is too heavy for thee; thou art not able to perform it thyself alone." "Thou wilt surely wear away," and he counseled Moses to appoint proper persons as rulers of thousands, and others as rulers of hundreds, and others of tens. They should be "able men, such as fear God, men of truth, hating covetousness." These were to judge in all matters of minor consequence, while the most difficult and important cases should still be brought before Moses, who was to be to the people, said Jethro, "to God-ward, that thou mayest bring the causes unto God: and thou shalt teach them ordinances and laws, and shalt show them the way wherein they must walk, and the work that they must do." This counsel was accepted, and it not only brought relief to Moses, but resulted in establishing more perfect order among the people.

The Lord had greatly honored Moses, and had wrought wonders by his hand; but the fact that he had been chosen to instruct others did not lead him to conclude that he himself needed no instruction. The chosen leader of Israel listened gladly to the suggestions of the godly priest of Midian, and adopted his plan as a wise arrangement.

From Rephidim the people continued their journey, following the movement of the cloudy pillar. Their route had led across barren plains, over steep ascents, and through rocky defiles. Often as they had traversed the sandy wastes, they had seen before them rugged mountains, like huge bulwarks, piled up directly across their course, and seeming to forbid all further progress. But as they approached, openings here and there appeared in the mountain wall, and beyond, another plain opened to view. Through one of the deep, gravelly passes they were now led. It was a grand and impressive scene. Between the rocky cliffs rising hundreds of feet on either side, flowed in a living tide, far as the eye could reach, the hosts of Israel with their flocks and herds. And now before them in solemn majesty Mount Sinai lifted its massive front. The cloudy pillar rested upon its summit, and the people spread their tents upon the plain beneath. Here was to be their home for nearly a year. At night the pillar of fire assured them of the divine protection, and while they were locked in slumber, the bread of heaven fell gently upon the encampment.

The dawn gilded the dark ridges of the mountains, and the sun's golden rays pierced the deep gorges, seeming to these weary travelers like beams of mercy from the throne of God. On every hand vast, rugged heights seemed in their solitary grandeur to speak of eternal endurance and majesty. Here the mind was impressed with solemnity and awe. Man was made to feel his ignorance and weakness in the presence of Him who "weighed the mountains in scales, and the hills in a balance." Isaiah 40:12. Here Israel was to receive the most wonderful revelation ever made by God to men. Here the Lord had gathered His people that He might impress upon them the sacredness of His requirements by declaring with His own voice His holy law. Great and radical changes were to be wrought in them; for the degrading influences of servitude and a long-continued association with idolatry had left their mark upon habits and character. God was working to lift them to a higher moral level by giving them a knowledge of Himself.

Chapter 8

This chapter is based on Exodus 19–24.

God Gives His Law to Israel

S oon after the encampment at Sinai, Moses was called up into the mountain to meet with God. Alone he climbed the steep and rugged path, and drew near to the cloud that marked the place of Jehovah's presence. Israel was now to be taken into a close and peculiar relation to the Most High—to be incorporated as a church and a nation under the government of God. The message to Moses for the people was:

> *Ye have seen what I did unto the Egyptians, and how I bare you on eagles' wings, and brought you unto Myself. Now therefore, if ye will obey My voice indeed, and keep My covenant, then ye shall be a peculiar treasure unto Me above all people: for all the earth is Mine: and ye shall be unto Me a kingdom of priests, and an holy nation.*

Moses returned to the camp, and having summoned the elders of Israel, he repeated to them the divine message. Their answer was, "All that the Lord hath spoken we will do." Thus they entered into a solemn covenant with God, pledging themselves to accept Him as their ruler, by which they became, in a special sense, the subjects of His authority.

Again their leader ascended the mountain, and the Lord said unto him, "Lo, I come unto thee in a thick cloud, that the people may hear when I speak with thee, and believe thee forever." When they met with difficulties in the way, they were disposed to murmur against Moses and Aaron, and accuse them of leading the hosts of Israel from Egypt to destroy them. The Lord would honor Moses before them, that they might be led to confide in his instructions.

God purposed to make the occasion of speaking His law a scene of awful grandeur, in keeping with its exalted character. The people were to be impressed that everything connected with the service of God must be regarded with the greatest reverence. The Lord said to Moses, "Go unto the people, and sanctify them to-day and tomorrow, and let them wash their clothes, and be ready against the third day: for the third day the Lord will come down in the sight of all the people upon Mount Sinai." During these intervening days all were to occupy the time in solemn preparation to appear before God. Their person and their clothing must be freed from impurity. And as Moses should point out their sins, they were to devote themselves to humiliation, fasting, and prayer, that their hearts might be cleansed from iniquity.

The preparations were made, according to the command; and in obedience to a further injunction, Moses directed that a barrier be placed about the mount, that neither man nor beast might intrude upon the sacred precinct. If any ventured so much as to touch it, the penalty was instant death.

On the morning of the third day, as the eyes of all the people were turned toward the mount, its summit was covered with a thick cloud, which grew more black and dense, sweeping downward until the entire mountain was wrapped in darkness and awful mystery. Then a sound as of a trumpet was heard, summoning the people to meet with God; and Moses led them forth to the base of the mountain. From the thick darkness flashed vivid lightnings, while peals of thunder echoed and re-echoed among the surrounding heights. "And Mount Sinai was altogether on a smoke, because the Lord descended upon it in fire: and the smoke thereof ascended as the smoke of a furnace, and the whole mount quaked greatly." "The glory of the Lord was like devouring fire on the top of the mount" in the sight of the assembled multitude. And "the voice of the trumpet sounded long, and waxed louder and louder." So terrible were the tokens of Jehovah's presence that the hosts of Israel shook with fear, and fell upon their faces before the Lord. Even Moses exclaimed, "I exceedingly fear and quake." Hebrews 12:21.

God's Voice Heard From Sinai

And now the thunders ceased; the trumpet was no longer heard; the earth was still. There was a period of solemn silence, and then the voice of God was heard. Speaking out of the thick darkness that enshrouded Him, as He stood upon the mount, surrounded by a retinue of angels, the Lord made known His law. Moses, describing the scene, says: "The Lord came from Sinai, and rose up from Seir unto them; He shined forth from Mount Paran, and He came with ten thousands of saints: from His right hand went a fiery law for them. Yea, He loved the people; all His saints are in Thy hand: and they sat down at Thy feet; every one shall receive of Thy words." Deuteronomy 33:2, 3.

Jehovah revealed Himself, not alone in the awful majesty of the judge and lawgiver, but as the compassionate guardian of His people: "I am the Lord thy God, which have brought thee out of the land of Egypt, out of the house of bondage." He whom they had already known as their Guide and Deliverer, who had brought them forth from Egypt, making a way for them through the sea, and overthrowing Pharaoh and his hosts, who had thus shown Himself to be above all the gods of Egypt—He it was who now spoke His law.

Whatever we cherish that tends to lessen our love for God ... of that do we make a god.

The law was not spoken at this time exclusively for the benefit of the Hebrews. God honored them by making them the guardians and keepers of His law, but it was to be held as a sacred trust for the whole world. The precepts of the Decalogue are adapted to all mankind, and they were given for the instruction and government of all. Ten precepts, brief, comprehensive, and authoritative, cover the duty of man to God and to his fellow man; and all based upon the great fundamental principle of love. "Thou shalt love the Lord thy God with all thy heart, and with all thy soul, and with all thy strength, and with all thy mind; and thy neighbor as thyself." Luke 10:27. See also Deuteronomy 6:4, 5; Leviticus 19:18. In the Ten Commandments these principles are carried out in detail, and made applicable to the condition and circumstances of man.

Thou shalt have no other gods before Me.

Jehovah, the eternal, self-existent, uncreated One, Himself the Source and Sustainer of all, is alone entitled to supreme reverence and worship. Man is forbidden to give to any other object the first place in his affections or his service. Whatever we cherish that tends to lessen our love for God or to interfere with the service due Him, of that do we make a god.

Thou shalt not make unto thee any graven image, or any likeness of anything that is in heaven above, or that is in the earth beneath, or that is in the water under the earth: thou shalt not bow down thyself to them, nor serve them.

The second commandment forbids the worship of the true God by images or similitudes. Many heathen nations claimed that their images were mere figures or symbols by which the Deity was worshiped, but God has declared such worship to be sin. The attempt to represent the Eternal One by material objects would lower man's conception of God. The mind, turned away from the infinite perfection of Jehovah, would be attracted to the creature rather than to the Creator. And as his conceptions of God were lowered, so would man become degraded.

> *The close and sacred relation of God to His people is represented under the figure of marriage.*
>
>

"I the Lord thy God am a jealous God." The close and sacred relation of God to His people is represented under the figure of marriage. Idolatry being spiritual adultery, the displeasure of God against it is fitly called jealousy.

"Visiting the iniquity of the fathers upon the children unto the third and fourth generation of them that hate Me." It is inevitable that children should suffer from the consequences of parental wrongdoing, but they are not punished for the parents' guilt, except as they participate in their sins. It is usually the case, however, that children walk in the steps of their parents. By inheritance and example the sons become partakers of the father's sin. Wrong tendencies, perverted appetites, and debased morals, as well as physical disease and degeneracy, are transmitted as a legacy from father to son, to the third and fourth generation. This fearful truth should have a solemn power to restrain men from following a course of sin.

"Showing mercy unto thousands of them that love Me, and keep My commandments." In prohibiting the worship of false gods, the second commandment by implication enjoins the worship of the true God. And to those who are faithful in His service, mercy is promised, not merely to the third and fourth generation as is the wrath threatened against those who hate Him, but to *thousands* of generations.

Thou shalt not take the name of the Lord thy God in vain: for the Lord will not hold him guiltless that taketh His name in vain.

This commandment not only prohibits false oaths and common swearing, but it forbids us to use the name of God in a light or careless manner, without regard to its awful significance. By the thoughtless mention of God in common conversation, by appeals to Him in trivial matters, and by the frequent and thoughtless repetition of His name, we dishonor Him. "Holy and reverend is His name." Psalm 111:9. All should meditate upon His majesty, His purity and holiness, that the heart may be impressed with a sense of His exalted character; and His holy name should be uttered with reverence and solemnity.

Remember the Sabbath day, to keep it holy. Six days shalt thou labor, and do all thy work: but the seventh day is the Sabbath of the Lord thy God: in it thou shalt not do any work, thou, nor thy son, nor thy daughter, thy manservant, nor thy maidservant, nor thy cattle, nor thy stranger that is within thy gates: for in six days the Lord made heaven and earth, the sea, and all that in them is, and rested the seventh day: wherefore the Lord blessed the Sabbath day, and hallowed it.

All who keep the seventh day signify by this act that they are worshipers of Jehovah.

The Sabbath is not introduced as a new institution but as having been founded at creation. It is to be remembered and observed as the memorial of the Creator's work. Pointing to God as the Maker of the heavens and the earth, it distinguishes the true God from all false gods. All who keep the seventh day signify by this act that they are worshipers of Jehovah. Thus the Sabbath is the sign of man's allegiance to God as long as there are any upon the earth to serve Him. The fourth commandment is the only one of all the ten in which are found both the name and the title of the Lawgiver. It is the only one that shows by whose authority the law is given. Thus it contains the seal of God, affixed to His law as evidence of its authenticity and binding force.

God has given men six days wherein to labor, and He requires that their own work be done in the six working days. Acts of necessity and mercy are permitted on the Sabbath, the sick and suffering are at all times to be cared for; but unnecessary labor is to be strictly avoided. "Turn away thy foot from the Sabbath, from doing thy pleasure on My holy day; and call the Sabbath a delight, the holy of the Lord, honorable; and ... honor Him, not doing thine own ways, nor finding thine own pleasure." Isaiah 58:13. Nor does the prohibition end here. "Nor speaking thine own words," says the prophet. Those who discuss business matters or lay plans on the Sabbath are regarded by God as though engaged in the actual transaction of business. To keep the Sabbath holy, we should not even allow our minds to dwell upon things of a worldly character. And the commandment includes all within our gates. The inmates of the house are to lay aside their worldly business during the sacred hours. All should unite to honor God by willing service upon His holy day.

Parents are entitled to a degree of respect which is due to no other person.

Honor thy father and thy mother: that thy days may be long upon the land which the Lord thy God giveth thee.

Parents are entitled to a degree of love and respect which is due to no other person. God Himself, who has placed upon them a responsibility for the souls committed to their charge, has ordained that during the earlier years of life, parents shall stand in the place of God to their children. And he who rejects the rightful authority of his parents is rejecting the authority of God. The fifth commandment requires children not only to yield respect, submission, and obedience to their parents, but also to give them love and tenderness, to lighten their cares, to guard their reputation, and to succor and comfort them in old age. It also enjoins respect for ministers and rulers and for all others to whom God has delegated authority.

This, says the apostle, "is the first commandment with promise." Ephesians 6:2. To Israel, expecting soon to enter Canaan, it was a pledge to the obedient, of long life in that good land; but it has a wider meaning, including all the Israel of God, and promising eternal life upon the earth when it shall be freed from the curse of sin.

Thou shalt not kill.

All acts of injustice that tend to shorten life; the spirit of hatred and revenge, or the indulgence of any passion that leads to injurious acts toward others, or causes us even to wish them harm (for "whosoever hateth his brother is a murderer"); a selfish neglect of caring for the needy or suffering; all self-indulgence or unnecessary deprivation or excessive labor that tends to injure health—all these are, to a greater or less degree, violations of the sixth commandment.

Thou shalt not commit adultery.

This commandment forbids not only acts of impurity, but sensual thoughts and desires, or any practice that tends to excite them. Purity is demanded not only in the outward life but in the secret intents and emotions of the heart. Christ, who taught the far-reaching obligation of the law of God, declared the evil thought or look to be as truly sin as is the unlawful deed.

An intention to deceive is what constitutes falsehood.

Thou shalt not steal.

Both public and private sins are included in this prohibition. The eighth commandment condemns manstealing and slave dealing, and forbids wars of conquest. It condemns theft and robbery. It demands strict integrity in the minutest details of the affairs of life. It forbids overreaching in trade, and requires the payment of just debts or wages. It declares that every attempt to advantage oneself by the ignorance, weakness, or misfortune of another is registered as fraud in the books of heaven.

Thou shalt not bear false witness against thy neighbor.

False speaking in any matter, every attempt or purpose to deceive our neighbor, is here included. An intention to deceive is what constitutes falsehood. By a glance of the eye, a motion of the hand, an expression of the countenance, a falsehood may be told as effectually as by words. All intentional overstatement, every hint or insinuation calculated to convey an erroneous or exaggerated impression, even the statement of facts in such a manner as to mislead, is falsehood. This precept forbids every effort to injure our neighbor's reputation by misrepresentation or evil surmising, by slander or tale bearing. Even the intentional suppression of truth, by which injury may result to others, is a violation of the ninth commandment.

Thou shalt not covet thy neighbor's house, thou shalt not covet thy neighbor's wife, nor his manservant, nor his maidservant, nor his ox, nor his ass, nor anything that is thy neighbor's.

The tenth commandment strikes at the very root of all sins, prohibiting the selfish desire, from which springs the sinful act. He who in obedience to God's law refrains from indulging even a sinful desire for that which belongs to another will not be guilty of an act of wrong toward his fellow creatures.

Israel's Response to the Lawgiver's Words

Such were the sacred precepts of the Decalogue, spoken amid thunder and flame, and with a wonderful display of the power and majesty of the great Lawgiver. God accompanied the proclamation of His law with exhibitions of His power and glory, that His people might never forget the scene, and that they might be impressed with profound veneration for the Author of the law, the Creator of heaven and earth. He would also show to all men the sacredness, the importance, and the permanence of His law.

The people of Israel were overwhelmed with terror. The awful power of God's utterances seemed more than their trembling hearts could bear. For as God's great rule of right was presented before them, they realized as never before the offensive character of sin, and their own guilt in the sight of a holy God. They shrank away from the mountain in fear and awe. The multitude cried out to Moses, "Speak thou with us, and we will hear: but let not God speak with us, lest we die." The leader answered, "Fear not: for God is come to prove you, and that His fear may be before your faces, that ye sin not." The people, however, remained at a distance, gazing in terror upon the scene, while Moses "drew near unto the thick darkness where God was."

The minds of the people, blinded and debased by slavery and heathenism, were not prepared to appreciate fully the far-reaching principles of God's ten precepts. That the obligations of the Decalogue might be more fully understood and enforced, additional precepts were given, illustrating and applying the principles of the Ten Commandments. These laws were called judgments, both because they were framed in infinite wisdom and equity and because the magistrates were to give judgment according to them. Unlike the Ten Commandments, they were delivered privately to Moses, who was to communicate them to the people.

The first of these laws related to servants. In ancient times criminals were sometimes sold into slavery by the judges; in some cases, debtors were sold by their creditors; and poverty even led persons to sell themselves or their children. But a Hebrew could not be sold as a slave for life. His term of service was limited to six years; on the seventh he was to be set at liberty. Manstealing, deliberate murder, and rebellion against parental authority were to be punished with death. The holding of slaves not of Israelitish birth was permitted, but their life and person were strictly guarded. The murderer of a slave was to be punished; an injury inflicted upon one by his master, though no more than the loss of a tooth, entitled him to his freedom.

The rights of widows and orphans were especially guarded.

The Israelites had lately been servants themselves, and now that they were to have servants under them, they were to beware of indulging the spirit of cruelty and exaction from which they had suffered under their Egyptian taskmasters. The memory of their own bitter servitude should enable them to put themselves in the servant's place, leading them to be kind and compassionate, to deal with others as they would wish to be dealt with.

The rights of widows and orphans were especially guarded, and a tender regard for their helpless condition was enjoined. "If thou afflict them in any wise," the Lord declared, "and they cry at all unto Me, I will surely hear their cry; and My wrath shall wax hot, and I will kill you with the sword; and your wives shall be widows, and your children fatherless." Aliens who united themselves with Israel were to be protected from wrong or oppression. "Thou shalt not oppress a stranger: for ye know the heart of a stranger, seeing ye were strangers in the land of Egypt."

While there were types pointing to a Savior to come, there was also a present Savior.

The taking of usury from the poor was forbidden. A poor man's raiment or blanket taken as a pledge, must be restored to him at nightfall. He who was guilty of theft was required to restore double. Respect for magistrates and rulers was enjoined, and judges were warned against perverting judgment, aiding a false cause, or receiving bribes. Calumny and slander were prohibited, and acts of kindness enjoined, even toward personal enemies.

Again the people were reminded of the sacred obligation of the Sabbath. Yearly feasts were appointed, at which all the men of the nation were to assemble before the Lord, bringing to Him their offerings of gratitude and the first fruits of His bounties. The object of all these regulations was stated: they proceeded from no exercise of mere arbitrary sovereignty; all were given for the good of Israel. The Lord said, "Ye shall be holy men unto Me"—worthy to be acknowledged by a holy God.

These laws were to be recorded by Moses, and carefully treasured as the foundation of the national law, and, with the ten precepts which they were given to illustrate, the condition of the fulfillment of God's promises to Israel.

The message was now given them from Jehovah: "Behold, I send an Angel before thee, to keep thee in the way, and to bring thee into the place which I have prepared. Beware of Him, and obey His voice, provoke Him not; for He will not pardon your transgressions: for My name is in Him. But if thou shalt indeed obey His voice, and do all that I speak; then I will be an enemy unto thine enemies, and an adversary unto thine adversaries." During all the wanderings of Israel, Christ, in the pillar of cloud and of fire, was their Leader. While there were types pointing to a Saviour to come, there was also a present Saviour, who gave commands to Moses for the people, and who was set forth before them as the only channel of blessing.

Upon descending from the mountain, "Moses came and told the people all the words of the Lord, and all the judgments: and all the people answered with one voice, and said, All the words which the Lord hath said will we do." This pledge, together with the words of the Lord which it bound them to obey, was written by Moses in a book.

Then followed the ratification of the covenant. An altar was built at the foot of the mountain, and beside it twelve pillars were set up, "according to the twelve tribes of Israel," as a testimony to their acceptance of the covenant. Sacrifices were then presented by young men chosen for the service.

Having sprinkled the altar with the blood of the offerings, Moses "took the book of the covenant, and read in the audience of the people." Thus the conditions of the covenant were solemnly repeated, and all were at liberty to choose whether or not they would comply with them. They had at the first promised to obey the voice of God; but they had since heard His law proclaimed; and its principles had been particularized, that they might know how much this covenant involved. Again the people answered with one accord, "All that the Lord hath said will we do, and be obedient." "When Moses had spoken every precept to all the people according to the law, he took the blood, …and sprinkled both the book and all the people, saying, This is the blood of the testament which God hath enjoined unto you." Hebrews 9:19, 20.

Israel Fully Established as a Nation

Arrangements were now to be made for the full establishment of the chosen nation under Jehovah as their king. Moses had received the command, "Come up unto the Lord, thou, and Aaron, Nadab, and Abihu, and seventy of the elders of Israel; and worship ye afar off. And Moses alone shall come near the Lord." While the people worshiped at its foot, these chosen men were called up into the mount. The seventy elders were to assist Moses in the government of Israel, and God put upon them His Spirit, and honored them with a view of His power and greatness. "And they saw the God of Israel: and there was under His feet as it were a paved work of a sapphire stone, and as it were the body of heaven in his clearness." They did not behold the Deity, but they saw the glory of His presence. Before this they could not have endured such a scene; but the exhibition of God's power had awed them to repentance; they had been contemplating His glory, purity, and mercy, until they could approach nearer to Him who was the subject of their meditations.

Moses and "his minister Joshua" were now summoned to meet with God. And as they were to be some time absent, the leader appointed Aaron and Hur, assisted by the elders, to act in his stead. "And Moses went up into the mount, and a cloud covered the mount. And the glory of the Lord abode upon Mount Sinai." For six days the cloud covered the mountain as a token of God's special presence; yet there was no revelation of Himself or communication of His will. During this time Moses remained in waiting for a summons to the presence chamber of the Most High. He had been directed, "Come up to Me into the mount, and be there," and though his patience and obedience were tested, he did not grow weary of watching, or forsake his post. This period of waiting was to him a time of preparation, of close self-examination. Even this favored servant of God could not at once approach into His presence and endure the exhibitions of His glory. Six days must be employed in devoting himself to God by searching of heart, meditation, and prayer before he could be prepared for direct communication with his Maker.

Upon the seventh day, which was the Sabbath, Moses was called up into the cloud. The thick cloud opened in the sight of all Israel, and the glory of the Lord broke forth like devouring fire. "And Moses went into the midst of the cloud, and gat him up into the mount; and Moses was in the mount forty days and forty nights." The forty days' tarry in the mount did not include the six days of preparation. During the six days Joshua was with Moses, and together they ate of the manna and drank of "the brook that descended out of the mount." But Joshua did not enter with Moses into the cloud. He remained without, and continued to eat and drink daily while awaiting the return of Moses, but Moses fasted during the entire forty days.

During his stay in the mount, Moses received directions for the building of a sanctuary in which the divine presence would be specially manifested. "Let them make Me a sanctuary; that I may dwell among them" (Exodus 25:8), was the command of God. For the third time the observance of the Sabbath was enjoined. "It is a sign between Me and the children of Israel forever," the Lord declared, "that ye may know that I am Jehovah that doth sanctify you. Ye shall keep the Sabbath therefore; for it is holy unto you. ...Whosoever doeth any work therein, that soul shall be cut off from among his people." Exodus 31:17, 13, 14. Directions had just been given for the immediate erection of the tabernacle for the service of God; and now the people might conclude, because the object had in view was the glory of God, and also because of their great need of a place of worship, that they would be justified in working at the building upon the Sabbath. To guard them from this error, the warning was given. Even the sacredness and urgency of that special work for God must not lead them to infringe upon His holy rest day.

Henceforth the people were to be honored with the abiding presence of their King. "I will dwell among the children of Israel, and will be their God," "and the tabernacle shall be sanctified by My glory" (Exodus 24:45, 43), was the assurance given to Moses. As the symbol of God's authority and the embodiment of His will, there was delivered to Moses a copy of the Decalogue engraved by the finger of God Himself upon two tables of stone (Deuteronomy 9:10; Exodus 32:15, 16), to be sacredly enshrined in the sanctuary, which, when made, was to be the visible center of the nation's worship.

From a race of slaves the Israelites had been exalted above all peoples to be the peculiar treasure of the King of kings. God had separated them from the world, that He might commit to them a sacred trust. He had made them the depositaries of His law, and He purposed, through them, to preserve among men the knowledge of Himself. Thus the light of heaven was to shine out to a world enshrouded in darkness, and a voice was to be heard appealing to all peoples to turn from their idolatry to serve the living God. If the Israelites would be true to their trust, they would become a power in the world. God would be their defense, and He would exalt them above all other nations. His light and truth would be revealed through them, and they would stand forth under His wise and holy rule as an example of the superiority of His worship over every form of idolatry.

Chapter 9

This chapter is based on Exodus 32–34.

Choosing to Please People Instead of Pleasing God

While Moses was absent it was a time of waiting and suspense to Israel. The people knew that he had ascended the mount with Joshua, and had entered the cloud of thick darkness which could be seen from the plain below, resting on the mountain peak, illuminated from time to time with the lightnings of the divine Presence. They waited eagerly for his return. Accustomed as they had been in Egypt to material representations of deity, it had been hard for them to trust in an invisible being, and they had come to rely upon Moses to sustain their faith. Now he was taken from them. Day after day, week after week passed, and still he did not return. Notwithstanding the cloud was still in view, it seemed to many in the camp that their leader had deserted them, or that he had been consumed by the devouring fire.

During this period of waiting, there was time for them to meditate upon the law of God which they had heard, and to prepare their hearts to receive the further revelations that He might make to them. They had none too much time for this work; and had they been thus seeking a clearer understanding of God's requirements, and humbling their hearts before Him, they would have been shielded from temptation. But they did not do this, and they soon became careless, inattentive, and lawless. Especially was this the case with the mixed multitude. They were impatient to be on their way to the Land of Promise—the land flowing with milk and honey. It was only on condition of obedience that the goodly land was promised them, but they had lost sight of this. There were some who suggested a return to Egypt, but whether forward to Canaan or backward to Egypt, the masses of the people were determined to wait no longer for Moses.

Feeling their helplessness in the absence of their leader, they returned to their old superstitions. The mixed multitude had been the first to indulge murmuring and impatience, and they were the leaders in the apostasy that followed. Among the objects regarded by the Egyptians as symbols of deity was the ox or calf; and it was at the suggestion of those who had practiced this form of idolatry in Egypt that a calf was now made and worshiped. The people desired some image to represent God, and to go before them in the place of Moses. God had given no manner of similitude of Himself, and He had prohibited any material representation for such a purpose. The mighty miracles in Egypt and at the Red Sea were designed to establish faith in Him as the invisible, all-powerful Helper of Israel, the only true God. And the desire for some visible manifestation of His presence had been granted in the pillar of cloud and of fire that guided their hosts, and in the revealing of His glory upon Mount Sinai. But with the cloud of the Presence still before them, they turned back in their hearts to the idolatry of Egypt, and represented the glory of the invisible God by the similitude of an ox!

In the absence of Moses, the judicial authority had been delegated to Aaron, and a vast crowd gathered about his tent, with the demand, "Make us gods, which shall go before us; for as for this Moses, the man that brought us up out of the land of Egypt, we wot not what is become of him." The cloud, they said, that had heretofore led them, now rested permanently upon the mount; it would no longer direct their travels. They must have an image in its place; and if, as had been suggested, they should decide to return to Egypt, they would find favor with the Egyptians by bearing this image before them and acknowledging it as their god.

Aaron Yields to the People's Demands

Such a crisis demanded a man of firmness, decision, and unflinching courage; one who held the honor of God above popular favor, personal safety, or life itself. But the present leader of Israel was not of this character. Aaron feebly remonstrated with the people, but his wavering and timidity at the critical moment only rendered them the more determined. The tumult increased. A blind, unreasoning frenzy seemed to take possession of the multitude. There were some who remained true to their covenant with God, but the greater part of the people joined in the apostasy. A few who ventured to denounce the proposed image making as idolatry, were set upon and roughly treated, and in the confusion and excitement they finally lost their lives.

Aaron feared for his own safety; and instead of nobly standing up for the honor of God, he yielded to the demands of the multitude. His first act was to direct that the golden earrings be collected from all the people and brought to him, hoping that pride would lead them to refuse such a sacrifice.

There are still pliant Aarons, who ... will yield to the desires of the unconsecrated.

But they willingly yielded up their ornaments; and from these he made a molten calf, in imitation of the gods of Egypt. The people proclaimed, "These be thy gods, O Israel, which brought thee up out of the land of Egypt." And Aaron basely permitted this insult to Jehovah. He did more. Seeing with what satisfaction the golden god was received, he built an altar before it, and made proclamation, "Tomorrow is a feast to the Lord." The announcement was heralded by trumpeters from company to company throughout the camp. "And they rose up early on the morrow, and offered burnt offerings, and brought peace offerings; and the people sat down to eat and to drink, and rose up to play." Under the pretense of holding "a feast to the Lord," they gave themselves up to gluttony and licentious reveling.

How often, in our own day, is the love of pleasure disguised by a "form of godliness!" A religion that permits men, while observing the rites of worship, to devote themselves to selfish or sensual gratification, is as pleasing to the multitudes now as in the days of Israel. And there are still pliant Aarons, who, while holding positions of authority in the church, will yield to the desires of the unconsecrated, and thus encourage them in sin.

Only a few days had passed since the Hebrews had made a solemn covenant with God to obey His voice. They had stood trembling with terror before the mount, listening to the words of the Lord, "Thou shalt have no other gods before Me." The glory of God still hovered above Sinai in the sight of the congregation; but they turned away, and asked for other gods. "They made a calf in Horeb, and worshiped the molten image. Thus they changed their glory into the similitude of an ox." Psalm 106:19, 20. How could greater ingratitude have been shown, or more daring insult offered, to Him who had revealed Himself to them as a tender father and an all-powerful king!

Moses in the mount was warned of the apostasy in the camp and was directed to return without delay. "Go, get thee down," were the words of God; "thy people, which thou broughtest out of the land of Egypt, have corrupted themselves: they have turned aside quickly out of the way which I commanded them. They have made them a molten calf, and have worshiped it." God might have checked the movement at the outset; but He suffered it to come to this height that He might teach all a lesson in His punishment of treason and apostasy.

God's covenant with His people had been disannulled, and He declared to Moses, "Let Me alone, that My wrath may wax hot against them, and that I may consume them: and I will make of thee a great nation." The people of Israel, especially the mixed multitude, would be constantly disposed to rebel against God. They would also murmur against their leader, and would grieve him by their unbelief and stubbornness, and it would be a laborious and soul-trying work to lead them through to the Promised Land. Their sins had already forfeited the favor of God, and justice called for their destruction. The Lord therefore proposed to destroy them, and make of Moses a mighty nation.

"Let Me alone, …that I may consume them," were the words of God. If God had purposed to destroy Israel, who could plead for them? How few but would have left the sinners to their fate! How few but would have gladly exchanged a lot of toil and burden and sacrifice, repaid with ingratitude and murmuring, for a position of ease and honor, when it was God Himself that offered the release.

> *Moses discerned ground for hope where there appeared only discouragement and wrath.*

But Moses discerned ground for hope where there appeared only discouragement and wrath. The words of God, "Let Me alone," he understood not to forbid but to encourage intercession, implying that nothing but the prayers of Moses could save Israel, but that if thus entreated, God would spare His people. He "besought the Lord his God, and said, Lord, why doth Thy wrath wax hot against Thy people, which Thou hast brought forth out of the land of Egypt with great power, and with a mighty hand?"

God had signified that He disowned His people. He had spoken of them to Moses as "*thy* people, which *thou* broughtest out of Egypt."

But Moses humbly disclaimed the leadership of Israel. They were not his, but God's—"*Thy* people, which *Thou* has brought forth ...with great power, and with a mighty hand. Wherefore," he urged, "should the Egyptians speak, and say, For mischief did He bring them out, to slay them in the mountains, and to consume them from the face of the earth?"

During the few months since Israel left Egypt, the report of their wonderful deliverance had spread to all the surrounding nations. Fear and terrible foreboding rested upon the heathen. All were watching to see what the God of Israel would do for His people. Should they now be destroyed, their enemies would triumph, and God would be dishonored. The Egyptians would claim that their accusations were true—instead of leading His people into the wilderness to sacrifice, He had caused them to be sacrificed. They would not consider the sins of Israel; the destruction of the people whom He had so signally honored, would bring reproach upon His name. How great the responsibility resting upon those whom God has highly honored, to make His name a praise in the earth! With what care should they guard against committing sin, to call down His judgments and cause His name to be reproached by the ungodly!

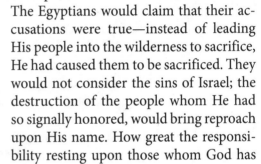

God had proved His servant; He had tested his faithfulness and his love for that erring, ungrateful people.

As Moses interceded for Israel, his timidity was lost in his deep interest and love for those for whom he had, in the hands of God, been the means of doing so much. The Lord listened to his pleadings, and granted his unselfish prayer. God had proved His servant; He had tested his faithfulness and his love for that erring, ungrateful people, and nobly had Moses endured the trial. His interest in Israel sprang from no selfish motive. The prosperity of God's chosen people was dearer to him than personal honor, dearer than the privilege of becoming the father of a mighty nation. God was pleased with his faithfulness, his simplicity of heart, and his integrity, and He committed to him, as a faithful shepherd, the great charge of leading Israel to the Promised Land.

As Moses and Joshua came down from the mount, the former bearing the "tables of the testimony," they heard the shouts and outcries of the excited multitude, evidently in a state of wild uproar. To

Joshua the soldier, the first thought was of an attack from their enemies. "There is a noise of war in the camp," he said. But Moses judged more truly the nature of the commotion. The sound was not that of combat, but of revelry. "It is not the voice of them that shout for mastery, neither is it the voice of them that cry for being overcome; but the noise of them that sing do I hear."

Israel Falls into Total Apostasy

As they drew near the encampment, they beheld the people shouting and dancing around their idol. It was a scene of heathen riot, an imitation of the idolatrous feasts of Egypt; but how unlike the solemn and reverent worship of God! Moses was overwhelmed. He had just come from the presence of God's glory, and though he had been warned of what was taking place, he was unprepared for that dreadful exhibition of the degradation of Israel. His anger was hot. To show his abhorrence of their crime, he threw down the tables of stone, and they were broken in the sight of all the people, thus signifying that as they had broken their covenant with God, so God had broken His covenant with them.

Entering the camp, Moses passed through the crowds of revelers, and seizing upon the idol, cast it into the fire. He afterward ground it to powder, and having strewed it upon the stream that descended from the mount, he made the people drink of it. Thus was shown the utter worthlessness of the god which they had been worshiping.

The great leader summoned his guilty brother and sternly demanded, "What did this people unto thee, that thou hast brought so great a sin upon them?" Aaron endeavored to shield himself by relating the clamors of the people; that if he had not complied with their wishes, he would have been put to death. "Let not the anger of my lord wax hot," he said; "thou knowest the people, that they are set on mischief. For they said unto me, Make us gods, which shall go before us: for as for this Moses, the man that brought us up out of the land of Egypt, we wot not what is become of him. And I said unto them, Whosoever hath any gold, let them break it off. So they gave it me: then I cast it into the fire, and there came out this calf." He would lead Moses to believe that a miracle had been wrought—that the gold had been cast into the fire, and by supernatural power changed to a calf.

But his excuses and prevarications were of no avail. He was justly dealt with as the chief offender.

The fact that Aaron had been blessed and honored so far above the people was what made his sin so heinous. It was Aaron "the saint of the Lord" (Psalm 106:16), that had made the idol and announced the feast. It was he who had been appointed as spokesman for Moses, and concerning whom God Himself had testified, "I know that he can speak well" (Exodus 4:14), that had failed to check the idolaters in their heaven-daring purpose. He by whom God had wrought in bringing judgments both upon the Egyptians and upon their gods, had heard unmoved the proclamation before the molten image, "These be thy gods, O Israel, which brought thee up out of the land of Egypt." It was he who had been with Moses on the mount, and had there beheld the glory of the Lord, who had seen that in the manifestation of that glory there was nothing of which an image could be made—it was he who had changed that glory into the similitude of an ox. He to whom God had committed the government of the people in the absence of Moses, was found sanctioning their rebellion. "The Lord was very angry with Aaron to have destroyed him." Deuteronomy 9:20. But in answer to the earnest intercession of Moses, his life was spared; and in penitence and humiliation for his great sin, he was restored to the favor of God.

> *Aaron's compliance with the desires of the people... emboldened them to go to greater lengths in sin.*
>
>

If Aaron had had courage to stand for the right, irrespective of consequences, he could have prevented that apostasy. If he had unswervingly maintained his own allegiance to God, if he had cited the people to the perils of Sinai, and had reminded them of their solemn covenant with God to obey His law, the evil would have been checked. But his compliance with the desires of the people and the calm assurance with which he proceeded to carry out their plans, emboldened them to go to greater lengths in sin than had before entered their minds.

When Moses, on returning to the camp, confronted the rebels, his severe rebukes and the indignation he displayed in breaking the sacred tables of the law were contrasted by the people with his brother's pleasant speech and dignified demeanor, and their sympathies were with Aaron. To justify himself, Aaron endeavored to make the people responsible for his weakness in yielding to their demand; but notwithstanding this, they were filled with admiration of his gentleness and patience. But God seeth not as man sees. Aaron's yielding spirit and his desire to please had blinded his eyes to the enormity of the crime he was sanctioning. His course in giving his influence to sin in Israel cost the life of thousands. In what contrast with this was the course of Moses, who, while faithfully executing God's judgments, showed that the welfare of Israel was dearer to him than prosperity or honor or life.

Punishment for Apostasy

Of all the sins that God will punish, none are more grievous in His sight than those that encourage others to do evil. God would have His servants prove their loyalty by faithfully rebuking transgression, however painful the act may be. Those who are honored with a divine commission are not to be weak, pliant time-servers. They are not to aim at self-exaltation, or to shun disagreeable duties, but to perform God's work with unswerving fidelity.

Though God had granted the prayer of Moses in sparing Israel from destruction, their apostasy was to be signally punished. The lawlessness and insubordination into which Aaron had permitted them to fall, if not speedily crushed, would run riot in wickedness, and would involve the nation in irretrievable ruin. By terrible severity the evil must be put away. Standing in the gate of the camp, Moses called to the people, "Who is on the Lord's side? let him come unto me." Those who had not joined in the apostasy were to take their position at the right of Moses; those who were guilty but repentant, at the left. The command was obeyed. It was found that the tribe of Levi had taken no part in the idolatrous worship. From among other tribes there were great numbers who, although they had sinned, now signified their repentance. But a large company, mostly of the mixed multitude that instigated the making of the calf, stubbornly persisted in their rebellion. In the name of "the Lord God of Israel," Moses now commanded those upon his right hand, who had kept themselves clear of idolatry, to gird on their swords and slay all who persisted in rebellion. "And there fell of the people that day about three thousand men." Without regard to position, kindred, or friendship, the ringleaders in wickedness were cut off; but all who repented and humbled themselves were spared.

Those who performed this terrible work of judgment were acting by divine authority, executing the sentence of the King of heaven. Men are to beware how they, in their human blindness, judge and condemn their fellow men; but when God commands them to execute His sentence upon iniquity, He is to be obeyed. Those who performed this painful act, thus manifested their abhorrence of rebellion and idolatry, and consecrated themselves more fully to the service of the true God. The Lord honored their faithfulness by bestowing special distinction upon the tribe of Levi.

> *That the divine government might be maintained justice must be visited upon the traitors. Yet even here God's mercy was displayed.*

The Israelites had been guilty of treason, and that against a King who had loaded them with benefits and whose authority they had voluntarily pledged themselves to obey. That the divine government might be maintained justice must be visited upon the traitors. Yet even here God's mercy was displayed. While He maintained His law, He granted freedom of choice and opportunity for repentance to all. Only those were cut off who persisted in rebellion.

It was necessary that this sin should be punished, as a testimony to surrounding nations of God's displeasure against idolatry. By executing justice upon the guilty, Moses, as God's instrument, must leave on record a solemn and public protest against their crime. As the Israelites should hereafter condemn the idolatry of the neighboring tribes, their enemies would throw back upon them the charge that the people who claimed Jehovah as their God had made a calf and worshiped it in Horeb. Then though compelled to acknowledge the disgraceful truth, Israel could point to the terrible fate of the transgressors, as evidence that their sin had not been sanctioned or excused.

Love no less than justice demanded that for this sin judgment should be inflicted. God is the guardian as well as the sovereign of His people. He cuts off those who are determined upon rebellion, that they may not lead others to ruin. In sparing the life of Cain,

God had demonstrated to the universe what would be the result of permitting sin to go unpunished. The influence exerted upon his descendants by his life and teaching led to the state of corruption that demanded the destruction of the whole world by a flood. The history of the antediluvians testifies that long life is not a blessing to the sinner; God's great forbearance did not repress their wickedness. The longer men lived, the more corrupt they became.

So with the apostasy at Sinai. Unless punishment had been speedily visited upon transgression, the same results would again have been seen. The earth would have become as corrupt as in the days of Noah. Had these transgressors been spared, evils would have followed, greater than resulted from sparing the life of Cain. It was the mercy of God that thousands should suffer, to prevent the necessity of visiting judgments upon millions. In order to save the many, He must punish the few. Furthermore, as the people had cast off their allegiance to God, they had forfeited the divine protection, and, deprived of their defense, the whole nation was exposed to the power of their enemies. Had not the evil been promptly put away, they would soon have fallen a prey to their numerous and powerful foes. It was necessary for the good of Israel, and also as a lesson to all succeeding generations, that crime should be promptly punished. And it was no less a mercy to the sinners themselves that they should be cut short in their evil course. Had their life been spared, the same spirit that led them to rebel against God would have been manifested in hatred and strife among themselves, and they would eventually have destroyed one another. It was in love to the world, in love to Israel, and even to the transgressors, that crime was punished with swift and terrible severity.

It was the mercy of God that thousands should suffer, to prevent the necessity of visiting judgment upon millions.

As the people were roused to see the enormity of their guilt, terror pervaded the entire encampment. It was feared that every offender was to be cut off. Pitying their distress, Moses promised to plead once more with God for them.

"Ye have sinned a great sin," he said, "and now I will go up unto the Lord; peradventure I shall make an atonement for your sin." He went, and in his confession before God he said, "Oh, this people have sinned a great sin, and have made them gods of gold. Yet now if Thou wilt forgive their sin—; and if not, blot me, I pray Thee, out of Thy book which Thou hast written." The answer was, "Whosoever hath sinned against Me, him will I blot out of My book. Therefore now go, lead the people into the place of which I have spoken unto thee: behold, Mine Angel shall go before thee: nevertheless, in the day when I visit, I will visit their sin upon them."

In the prayer of Moses our minds are directed to the heavenly records in which the names of all men are inscribed, and their deeds, whether good or evil, are faithfully registered. The book of life contains the names of all who have ever entered the service of God. If any of these depart from Him, and by stubborn persistence in sin become finally hardened against the influences of His Holy Spirit, their names will in the judgment be blotted from the book of life, and they themselves will be devoted to destruction. Moses realized how dreadful would be the fate of the sinner; yet if the people of Israel were to be rejected by the Lord, he desired his name to be blotted out with theirs; he could not endure to see the judgments of God fall upon those who had been so graciously delivered. The intercession of Moses in behalf of Israel illustrates the mediation of Christ for sinful men. But the Lord did not permit Moses to bear, as did Christ, the guilt of the transgressor. "Whosoever hath sinned against Me," He said, "him will I blot out of My book."

The intercession of Moses in behalf of Israel illustrates the mediation of Christ for sinful men.

In deep sadness the people had buried their dead. Three thousand had fallen by the sword; a plague had soon after broken out in the encampment; and now the message came to them that the divine Presence would no longer accompany them in their journeyings. Jehovah had declared, "I will not go up in the midst of thee; for thou art a stiffnecked people: lest I consume thee in the way." And the command was given, "Put off thy ornaments from thee, that I may know what to do unto thee." Now there was mourning throughout the encampment. In penitence and humiliation "the children of Israel stripped themselves of their ornaments by the mount Horeb."

By the divine direction the tent that had served as a temporary place of worship was removed "afar off from the camp." This was still further evidence that God had withdrawn His presence from them. He would reveal Himself to Moses, but not to such a people. The rebuke was keenly felt, and to the conscience-smitten multitudes it seemed a foreboding of greater calamity. Had not the Lord separated Moses from the camp that He might utterly destroy them? But they were not left without hope. The tent was pitched without the encampment, but Moses called it "the tabernacle of the congregation." All who were truly penitent, and desired to return to the Lord, were directed to repair thither to confess their sins and seek His mercy. When they returned to their tents Moses entered the tabernacle. With agonizing interest the people watched for some token that his intercessions in their behalf were accepted. If God should condescend to meet with him, they might hope that they were not to be utterly consumed. When the cloudy pillar descended, and stood at the entrance of the tabernacle, the people wept for joy, and they "rose up and worshiped, every man in his tent door."

Moses had learned that in order to prevail with the people, he must have help from God.

Moses knew well the perversity and blindness of those who were placed under his care; he knew the difficulties with which he must contend. But he had learned that in order to prevail with the people, he must have help from God. He pleaded for a clearer revelation of God's will and for an assurance of His presence: "See, Thou sayest unto me, Bring up this people: and Thou hast not let me know whom Thou wilt send with me. Yet Thou hast said, I know thee by name, and thou hast also found grace in My sight. Now therefore, I pray Thee, if I have found grace in Thy sight, show me now Thy way, that I may know Thee, that I may find grace in Thy sight: and consider that this nation is Thy people."

The answer was, "My presence shall go with thee, and I will give thee rest." But Moses was not yet satisfied. There pressed upon his soul a sense of the terrible results should God leave Israel to hardness and impenitence. He could not endure that his interests should be separated from those of his brethren, and he prayed that the favor of God might be restored to His people, and that the token of His presence might continue to direct their journeyings: "If Thy presence go not with me, carry us not up hence. For wherein shall it be known here that I and Thy people have found grace in Thy sight? is it not in that Thou goest with us? So shall we be separated, I and Thy people, from all the people that are upon the face of the earth."

And the Lord said, "I will do this thing also that thou hast spoken: for thou hast found grace in My sight, and I know thee by name." Still the prophet did not cease pleading. Every prayer had been answered, but he thirsted for greater tokens of God's favor. He now made a request that no human being had ever made before: "I beseech Thee, show me Thy glory."

God did not rebuke his request as presumptuous; but the gracious words were spoken, "I will make all My goodness pass before thee." The unveiled glory of God, no man in this mortal state can look upon and live; but Moses was assured that he should behold as much of the divine glory as he could endure. Again he was summoned to the mountain summit; then the hand that made the world, that hand that "removeth the mountains, and they know not" (Job 9:5), took this creature of the dust, this mighty man of faith, and placed him in a cleft of the rock, while the glory of God and all His goodness passed before him.

This experience—above all else the promise that the divine Presence would attend him—was to Moses an assurance of success in the work before him; and he counted it of infinitely greater worth than all the learning of Egypt or all his attainments as a statesman or a military leader. No earthly power or skill or learning can supply the place of God's abiding presence.

To the transgressor it is a fearful thing to fall into the hands of the living God; but Moses stood alone in the presence of the Eternal One, and he was not afraid; for his soul was in harmony with the will of his Maker. Says the psalmist, "If I regard iniquity in my heart, the Lord will not hear me." Psalm 66:18. But "the secret of the Lord is with them that fear Him; and He will show them His covenant." Psalm 25:14.

The Deity proclaimed Himself, "The Lord, The Lord God, merciful and gracious, long-suffering, and abundant in goodness and truth, keeping mercy for thousands, forgiving iniquity and transgression and sin, and that will by no means clear the guilty."

"Moses made haste, and bowed his head toward the earth, and worshiped." Again he entreated that God would pardon the iniquity of His people, and take them for His inheritance. His prayer was granted. The Lord graciously promised to renew His favor to Israel, and in their behalf to do marvels such as had not been done "in all the earth, nor in any nation."

Moses Spends 40 Days and Nights on the Mount

Forty days and nights Moses remained in the mount; and during all this time, as at the first, he was miraculously sustained. No man had been permitted to go up with him, nor during the time of his absence were any to approach the mount. At God's command he had prepared two tables of stone, and had taken them with him to the summit; and again the Lord "wrote upon the tables the words of the covenant, the Ten Commandments."

During that long time spent in communion with God, the face of Moses had reflected the glory of the divine Presence; unknown to himself his face shown with a dazzling light when he descended from the mountain. Such a light illumined the countenance of Stephen when brought before his judges; "and all that sat in the council, looking steadfastly on him, saw his face as it had been the face of an angel." Acts 6:15. Aaron as well as the people shrank away from Moses, and "they were afraid to come nigh him." Seeing their confusion and terror, but ignorant of the cause, he urged them to come near. He held out to them the pledge of God's reconciliation, and assured them of His restored favor. They perceived in his voice nothing but love and entreaty, and at last one ventured to approach him. Too awed to speak, he silently pointed to the countenance of Moses, and then toward heaven. The great leader understood his meaning. In their conscious guilt, feeling themselves still under the divine displeasure, they could not endure the heavenly light, which, had they been obedient to God, would have filled them with joy. There is fear in guilt. The soul that is free from sin will not wish to hide from the light of heaven.

Moses had much to communicate to them; and compassionating their fear, he put a veil upon his face, and continued to do so thereafter whenever he returned to the camp from communion with God.

By this brightness God designed to impress upon Israel the sacred, exalted character of His law, and the glory of the gospel revealed through Christ. While Moses was in the mount, God presented to him, not only the tables of the law, but also the plan of salvation. He saw that the sacrifice of Christ was pre-figured by all the types and symbols of the Jewish age; and it was the heavenly light streaming from Calvary, no less than the glory of the law of God, that shed such a radiance upon the face of Moses. That divine illumination symbolized the glory of the dispensation of which Moses was the visible mediator, a representative of the one true Intercessor.

The glory reflected in the countenance of Moses illustrates the blessings to be received by God's commandment-keeping people through the mediation of Christ. It testifies that the closer our communion with God, and the clearer our knowledge of His requirements, the more fully shall we be conformed to the divine image, and the more readily do we become partakers of the divine nature.

Moses was a type of Christ. As Israel's intercessor veiled his countenance, because the people could not endure to look upon its glory, so Christ, the divine Mediator, veiled His divinity with humanity when He came to earth. Had He come clothed with the brightness of heaven, he could not have found access to men in their sinful state. They could not have endured the glory of His presence. Therefore He humbled Himself, and was made "in the likeness of sinful flesh" (Romans 8:3), that He might reach the fallen race, and lift them up.

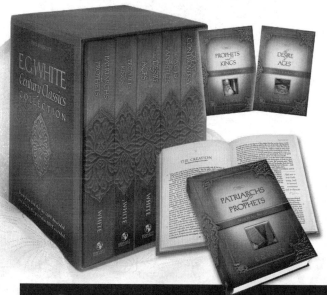

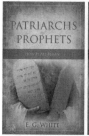   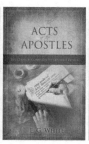